"Durability, Efficien

Extracts from a manual of kitch

Mary Eleanor Blakey

late of Bowthorpe Hall near Selby.

The author, aged about 8, from a studio portrait taken in Scarborough in the 1880s.
Courtesy of the Blakey archive

Discovered in a charity shop reject pile in Selby in 2012. Edited along with additional information on Mary's life and times, by David Lewis.

Published by David Lewis at 32 Church End, Cawood, Selby, YO8 3SN dglmeb @gmail.com

Printed by Axis Printing, Unit 10, Brookfoot Business Park, Elland Road, Brighouse, West Yorkshire HD6 2SD

Contents

Household Hints

1. Cakes will not stick to their tins if placed on a damp cloth when removed from the oven.
2. Cover a custard while cooling and a thick skin will not form on the top.
3. Green vegetables preserve their colour better if they are boiled rapidly and left uncovered.

Introduction

A mundane Monday in a charity shop in Selby.

'A battered, tatty old green notebook'

I was 'on the books'. That is, sorting through piles of donated books. Those in good condition are put to one side, priced up and put on the shelves.

Those remaining in the pile of tired, dog-eared, tea-stained, defaced volumes have only one further journey in life : the shredder!

With anything like that, there's no time to think - just lob it across the table, into the book bin and ultimately off to be pulped, earning about 10p per kilo for the charity.

Dan Brown? That'll sell.   Martina Cole? Fine.   Jeremy Clarkson? Maybe.

A battered, tatty old green notebook? No chance !

Toss it across the table ready to meet its fate at the teeth of the mulching and chomping machines. Off she goes !!

Only my aim wasn't true - and the book hit the side of the bin.

It fell open on the floor - and at once the wonderful contents were displayed.

Pages of recipes in a painstaking copperplate script, ruled off authoritatively in red ink, lay exposed to view.

How could you recycle a book containing pages like this ?

Baked Haddock & Brown Sauce.
Irish Stew.
Sago Pudding

Baked Stuffed Haddock. ½ Teasp: dried Thyme
1 Haddock 2½ to 3 lbs. in weight. 3 Tablesp: milk
3 ozs old bread (crusts) Little cold water
1½ " finely chopped suet. ½ teas. salt
2 tablesp: finely " parsley ¼ " pepper.
Method
Clean scrape and trim the fish. Take out the eyes
wash and wipe it. Soak the bread in the milk
and water until soft. Drain all the liquid from it,
and beat it up quite fine with a fork. Add the
suet, herbs and seasoning, and stuff the inside of
the fish with it. Sew or skewer it up. Put the tail
through the eyeholes, fasten with a skewer. Make 2 ozs
of dripping hot in a tin, put in the haddock, dredge
with flour, & bake. Allow about ¼ hr. to each lb. Baste
well. Dish up and serve with brown Sauce.
Brown Sauce.
½ oz butter. 1 Tables. flour. ½ pt. fish stock or water. Salt.
½ tablesp: vinegar. A few drops of browning.
Melt butter in a pan, add flour, then gradually the water, stir until
it boils. Cook well. Pour away any fat from the tin, pour the sauce into
the tin, Add vinegar, if necess. more browning & salt. Strain & it
is ready.

Of course you couldn't, so the book was rescued from the pile and put to one side for further investigation. Seldom has a tea-break been so eagerly awaited!

The author proudly announces herself on the title page of the book :

Mary Eleanor Blakey.

April 21st 1903.

Back in 2012, that name meant nothing to me, but with the help of friends, family members, those who work with and research archives and family and local history enthusiasts, I feel I now have a good understanding of who Mary Eleanor was and what kind of life she led. I'm still investigating her life, but after almost four years, it seemed timely to publish what has been discovered about the book's author and to share her century-old culinary wisdom.

My adaption of her book begins with an outline of her varied life before considering her classes, her meals, her kitchen regime and finally how her work sits in the world of that time. Those who gave invaluable help, along with book and internet references are listed in the final chapter.

But, after all that research, why are extracts of her book so worthy of publication?

Leaving aside the wonderfully random manner of its discovery, the quality and clarity of her script is a joy in itself.

Turning past her inscription, one comes upon four pages of wonderfully varied contents. A page on Meat and Vegetables is followed by one on Cakes, Puddings and Fish followed by Sauces, Soups and Pastries and finally Miscellaneous. Some of this classification may seem a little unusual. For instance bread is listed under "Cakes" and Porridge is listed under "Puddings", but there is clear evidence of someone who at the age of 27 can organize information in a way that is both appropriate and effective.

Investigating those four pges of recipes reveals many - Irish Stew and Teacakes for example - that are familiar to us today, but some that either sound unusual, like Black Cap and Cheap Cabinet Puddings or hark back to the days when a housewife had to make full use of all sources of protein. Cases in point are recipes for Battered Tripe and Stuffed Sheep's Heart.

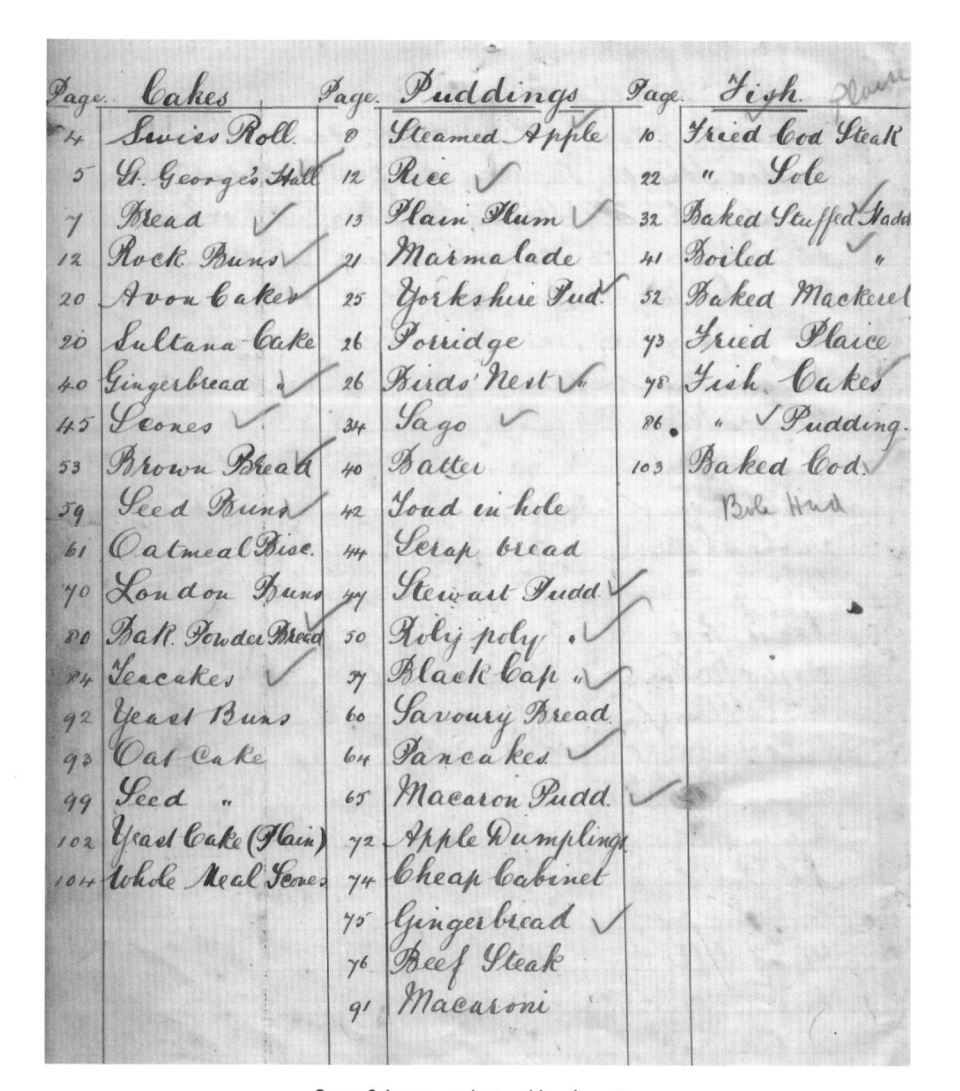

Page	Cakes	Page	Puddings	Page	Fish
4	Swiss Roll	8	Steamed Apple	10	Fried Cod Steak
5	St. George's Hall	12	Rice	22	" Sole
7	Bread	13	Plain Plum	32	Baked Stuffed Hadd
12	Rock Buns	21	Marmalade	41	Boiled "
20	Avon Cakes	25	Yorkshire Pud.	52	Baked Mackerel
20	Sultana Cake	26	Porridge	73	Fried Plaice
40	Gingerbread	26	Birds' Nest	78	Fish Cakes
45	Scones	34	Sago	86	" Pudding
53	Brown Bread	40	Batter	103	Baked Cod
59	Seed Buns	42	Toad in hole		Brk Hud
61	Oatmeal Bisc.	44	Scrap bread		
70	London Buns	44	Stewart Pudd.		
80	Bak. Powder Bread	50	Roly poly		
84	Teacakes	57	Black Cap		
92	Yeast Buns	60	Savoury Bread		
93	Oat Cake	64	Pancakes		
99	Seed "	65	Macaron Pudd.		
102	Yeast Cake (Plain)	72	Apple Dumpling		
104	Whole Meal Scones	74	Cheap Cabinet		
		75	Gingerbread		
		76	Beef Steak		
		91	Macaroni		

One of the pages listing Mary's recipes

Perhaps more importantly, notes at the back of the book showed that not only was Mary a fine cook and kitchen manager but that she was also far-sighted in her use of that knowledge. Mary not only recorded her recipes, but also organized some of them into a course of 19 lessons for '*Factory Girls, Domestic Servants*' and *Labourers' Daughters* to be delivered at evening classes. This planning showed Mary was a very well-organized and forward-thinking woman.

Finally, the book is quite a historical document in itself. Not only in terms of referring to foods we would no longer consider, but also in the way that a kitchen has to be managed.

In Mary's 'scullery' section there's an in-depth diagram of the innards of the coal-fired range, instructions on how to keep the tines of your forks pin-prick sharp, and the how and why of cleansing the U bend of the kitchen sink. Marvellously practical advice from more than a century ago!

Also in this section, Mary described the attributes of a good kitchen stove as **"durability, efficiency, economy"**. I've taken that phrase of hers to be the title of this book, encapsulating as it does her approach to thriftily-produced yet nourishing food from a 'modern' kitchen.

Since, in my opinion, the book is so good, a final question might be to wonder why her cookbook has not just been published in its entirety.

There are some repetitions : for instance, there are three very similar meat stews, and some of the recipes themselves are written twice, on different pages. Also several of the cakes and puddings are minor variants on the theme of flour, fat, breadcrumbs and dried fruit. Therefore I thought it would be of greater interest to take a selection of Mary's recipes and advice, and add notes putting her work into historical, educational and culinary contexts.

This book contains around 70 of her recipes along with her kitchen advice. I haven't tried all of them, so cannot vouch for their quality, and in the light of modern concerns about food safety, some of the recipes linked to bones and offal may not be considered safe.

But, bearing that in mind, I hope you read the book with interest and that you're inspired to at least try some of the recipes.

Perhaps a few people still use recipes handed down through the family on scraps of paper. An even luckier few may still have a granny who cooks 'the way it used to be'. But to have a cookbook with over 150 recipes, written out in scrupulous copperplate script, along with hints on kitchen management and a fully detailed syllabus of how to teach it all at Evening Class? That's quite a find!

It was a joy to have discovered Mary's book. It has been a further joy to research her life and meet so many people who have been so helpful on that journey. Hopefully a little of that joy can spread to you as you read of her life and her kitchen experience.

A note about Mary's recipes

When Mary began to write her cookbook, it was composed to meet the needs of that time, and in a style her students would understand. The precise data-driven detail one might expect today is not present. Back in 1903, Mary expected her students to have a 'feel', for example, for cooking temperatures and times.

Thus, when she writes of a 'slow' oven, that would mean one that would cook slowly, i.e. a cool one. Conversely, a "quick" oven would be a hot one, so a moderate one would be somewhere in between.

Some of her measures are antiquated and regional, too. A "gill" is a ¼ pint, a "cup" is about ½ pint and a quart is 2 pints. At other times her measure are wilfully vague, so in the recipe for "Moggy" she refers to a "handful of sugar". I have not attempted to metricate Mary's measurements.

In essence whilst Mary is trying to guide her students to prepare a wider range of meals, she also expects her trainee chefs to have the common cooking sense they've gained at their mother's side. This also holds true in some of her detais, when she doesn't tell you exactly when to grate the nutmeg or add the salt : it is assumed you know such things.

Some of her choice of ingredients reflect the energy intake required by physical labourers. Modern tastes may want to substitute lower-cholesterol fat for the butter or lard that she stipulates,

Finally, please note that in Edwardian Yorkshire cooking, what Mary describes as "treacle" we would today call golden syrup. The context of her references to "flour" imply plain flour is to be used, as she often has baking powder in her recipes as well. If you only have self-raising, the don't add baking powder.

Examples of Edwardian metal measuring jugs and pans

Who was Mary Eleanor Blakey?

Mary's cookbook is beautifully and eloquently-written : but what is her own story?

The obvious place to begin the search would have been to look at the donation bag in which the book had arrived, to trace the donor. Sadly, by the time the quality of the book had been realised, the other contributions from that bag had been thoroughly mixed up with donations from other sources, so it was not possible to go back to the pile of goods with any certainty to find any clues there.

The next thought was to search the cookbook itself. Unfortunately, again, this wasn't much help! Apart from the date and signature on the title page and a sticker from E.J. Arnold, the Leeds' stationer, on the inside cover, there were no identifying features. There were modern notes about the history of Hemingbrough and Osgodby, villages close to Selby, in a different script, in the middle of the book. With its donation to a Selby charity shop, some kind of link to Selby seemed probable.

The title page showed the book was begun in 1903, so Mary must have been old enough by then to have learnt how to cook well, to take care of kitchen equipment and be mature enough to be able to plan and deliver Domestic Science lessons. In the light of this, a birth date before 1880 seemed likely.

Ripon and Ripley

Guessing she must have been a Yorkshire lass, a search for "Mary Eleanor Blakey" was made in census and birth records. Local publicity included an article in 'Down Your Way' magazine, which resulted in several suggestions. From these, the best fit for the Mary who wrote the book seemed to be a child born on 9th April 1876 to parents residing in the parish of Clint, lying in fertile farmland to the south west of Ripon.

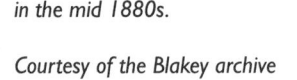

Mary's father, Thomas and mother, Sarah.

Portraits possibly taken in Scarborough in the mid 1880s.

Courtesy of the Blakey archive

Building on this assumption, I have tried to elucidate the story of Mary, the third child and eldest daughter of farmers Thomas and Sarah Blakey, part of a family that eventually numbered nine children. In discussion with modern-day members of the Blakey family, it is understood that the family had been tenant farmers in this area of Ripon since the mid-18th century. In the 1841 census, Mary's great grandfather is listed as being at Whipley Lane Farm, in the parish of Clint, which lies on a minor road just west of Ripley Castle. This is on the Ingleby's estate, a family which had controlled much of the land in the area since the 14th century. It is possible that Thomas and Sarah were living at Whipley Lane when Mary was born.

Tenant farmers did not have a lot of security of tenure : the farmer might want to move to a farm with more productive land, or the landlord might change the terms of the lease. For whatever reasons, Mary's time in the parish of Clint was brief, as by the 1881 census the family had moved a few miles to the neighbouring parish of Markington to work land close to historic Fountains Abbey and the Grade II-listed Markington Hall, home to the Wilberforce family of anti-slavery fame.

The Blakey home was Hincks Hall Farm, itself a listed building, parts of which date back to 1664. The Farm still exists today, a substantial farmhouse, with several attractive stone outbuildings around the farmyard. A list of tenants is held there, including the Blakey's tenure. Who or what Hincks was remains a mystery, but clearly someone or something of note, as a nearby wood also bears the name.

You can walk in Mary's footsteps on the track past the farm, as part of the 'Ripon Rowel' walk. The farm comprised around 150 acres, probably a mixed arable and livestock undertaking. The Blakey family clearly had some standing, as census returns show that they employed two labourers and a servant to assist in running the farm. During the family's stay at Hincks Hall, more children were born to Thomas and Sarah, including brother Andrew Hebden Blakey, who was to play several pivotal roles in his elder sister's life.

Hincks Hall Farm is one of many isolated properties that the Blakeys occupied, but it does lie on a network of footpaths that connect to nearby villages, road and rail links. For instance, the major north-south road, now the A61 that joins Harrogate and Ripon, is only a couple of miles distant, and two railway lines were similarly placed. Markington Crossing, on the Leeds to Thirsk railway, was less than a mile by footpath from Hincks Hall, with Wormald Green station a further mile away. Hampsthwaite and Birstwith stations on the Nidd Valley railway, linking Pateley Bridge, Harrogate and Knaresborough were equally close to Clint [see map p.10]

Whilst the Blakeys had farmed in the area for over a century, transport routes were thus available for tenant farmers like them to move out of the district should a better offer arise. In subsequent years, the Blakeys took advantage of these corridors.

8

(Above) : A view across the parish of Clint in the Nidd valley from the hamlet of Clint
(Below) : Hincks Hall Farm in 2014, with the path to Markington to the right of the house

Carved lintel over Hincks Hall Farm's front door reading "16 THE 64"

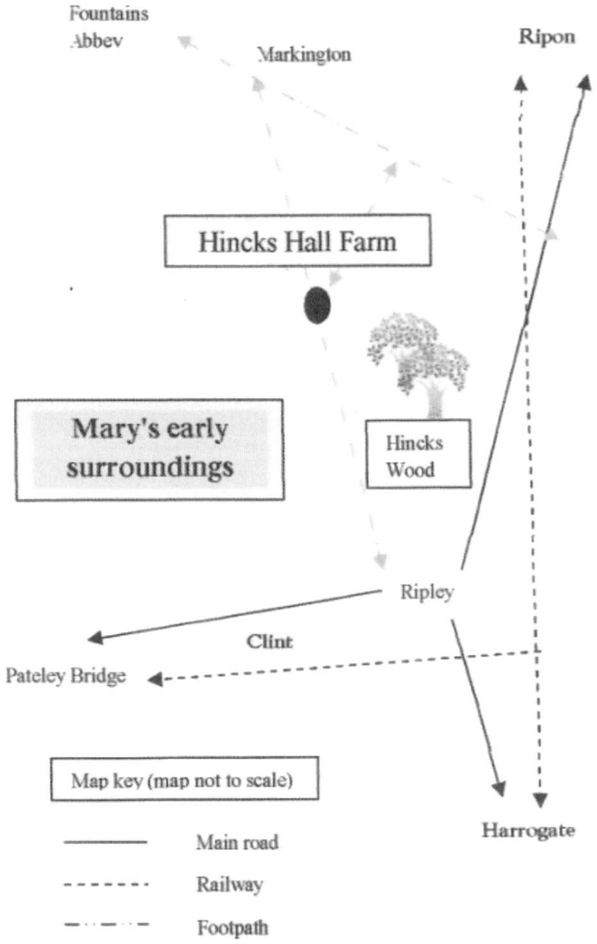

Fountains
Abbev   Markington   Ripon

Hincks Hall Farm

Mary's early
surroundings   Hincks
Wood

Ripley

Clint

Pateley Bridge

Map key (map not to scale)

————   Main road

- - - - - -   Railway

— · · — · · —   Footpath

Harrogate

Howden

By the time of the 1891 census, the family had moved forty miles or so to new surroundings in search of better pastures. Their journey was from the West Riding, to the East Riding market town of Howden where they settled at Wood Lane Farm, between the town of Howden and North Howden station. This farm land is now houses. Howden was also served by the Hull and Barnsley Railway, and their line crossed the Howden to Selby Road close to Park Farm, which was occupied by another branch of the Blakey family. This level crossing was called 'Selby Road Crossing', but after the line closed in 1968 the land stood empty. When the railway land was finally redeveloped for housing in the early 21st century, a century after the family had farmed there, the road adjoining the Selby Road was named 'Blakey's Crossing'. However, this name seems to refer to an unrelated Arthur Blakey who had a house and smallholding on the site until 1947.

Junction of Blakeys Crossing and Selby Road, Howden, 2014

Over the passage of another 10 years, the Blakey family made further moves. Mary's brother John kept on the family farm in Howden, whilst her parents moved to the 18-roomed Bowthorpe Hall near the River Derwent, around eight miles east of Selby and a similar distance to the west of Howden. The Hall and adjoining farm were of a similar size to Hincks Hall and the land possibly more fertile. It is also as isolated, if not more so, than Hincks, being cut off to the east by the river, and with only minor roads leading to the small settlements of South Duffield, Hemingbrough and Menthorpe, although the latter two were served by the railway.

Bowthorpe Hall in a watercolour from 1929 by J.W. Gibson. Courtesy of the Blakey archive

Leaving the family home

In the meantime, Mary had left the nest. The 1901 census shows her lodging with the family of Levi Rowley, a colliery lamp cleaner in Rothwell, a mining village to the south-east of Leeds. Levi was a former miner who, presumably due to injury, now had a surface job at one of the pits in the Rothwell area. This was relatively poorly paid, so the family would have welcomed Mary as a lodger for both financial and culinary reasons. Levi's wife Mary and daughter Henrietta also resided at the small terraced house, 2 Steel's Terrace, the name derived from the builder. Modern road signs refer to 'Steel Terrace' : whatever the name, the row of five houses still exists.

Whilst the bricks and mortar survive, Mary would not recognize the surroundings.

Back Gillet Lane (Gillet also has a variable spelling : in some places one 't', in others two), to the rear of the terrace on the photo, leads to Steel Terrace and was a rough track, but is now properly metalled.

What was once an area of waste ground no longer welcomes Rothwell Feast and other attractions that Mary would have enjoyed every Easter time, but instead hosts flats built in the 1960s that now hem in Steel Terrace. Rothwell Beck still runs at the bottom of the garden, but the hillside beyond, which Mary would have seen as market gardens, is now cut by a through road, Park West, and has been developed into a housing estate.

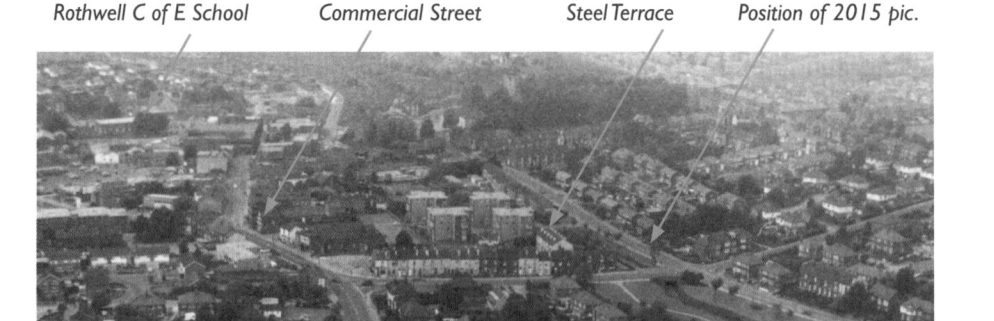

Steel Terrace (white, centre), Rothwell Beck, and Park West (extreme right) from Gillet Lane, 2015

It was whilst living in Rothwell in 1903 that Mary began her book. She was in her mid-20s and an Assistant Mistress at the local Church of England school. In such a position, it was vital for Mary to present her work on the blackboard in meticulous style, and from the evidence of the cookbook it is clear that she did. Her work at the school must also have enabled her to use the premises for the Evening Classes she devised and ran. These classes are discussed in more detail in chapter 7.

Rothwell C of E School   Commercial Street   Steel Terrace   Position of 2015 pic.

pre-1970s aerial view of Rothwell . Courtesy of the 'Rothwell Record'

13

Mary would have had a short walk to school from her lodgings, via the central shopping area of Rothwell, Commercial Street, to her school at the far end of this street. The building that Mary knew was demolished to make way for a supermarket in the early 1970s. A new school which still serves the town was built at another site.

Return to the family

We do not know exactly when or why Mary ventured to Rothwell. Perhaps as the eldest girl in the family, it was felt that it was time for her to make her way in the world. However, family events over the next five years meant a return to the East Riding. Mary's father Thomas died in a Scarborough nursing home in 1904, and her mother Sarah followed in 1906. Perhaps brother Andrew moved to Bowthorpe, and perhaps Mary might have been in charge of domestic arrangements there, although Thomas and Sarah did have servants. Younger brother John had now married and was living in Howden, so Mary may have lodged at Wood Lane. In truth, Mary's whereabouts are uncertain until her wedding in 1909, the next part of her story.

The lure of the sheep pen

Mary's future husband, James William Hall (usually known as William or Willie) was a farmer and a draper, living in Cockermouth, Cumberland. They seem an unlikely pair: whilst both are from farming stock, Willie was several years older than Mary, as well as being around 200 miles distant.

Mary's brother Andrew may well have been the conduit for the connection. Andrew was renowned locally as the 'cattle king' with a good eye for rearing sheep. William was celebrated in Cumberland as a breeder of champion Border Leicester sheep, well known for improving the bloodlines of other flocks, and Shorthorn cattle. Andrew was famed as a man who struck a hard bargain; William was renowned throughout the Borders for his skill in assessing the value of property and was a highly respected judge at agricultural shows. Two men with driven personalities and a common interest. How could they come to meet?

A major sheep fair would surely be the ideal venue. Such an event, one of the largest in the country, took place annually in September in Masham, near the Blakey's old stomping ground of Ripon, but more crucially perhaps, about halfway between Cockermouth and Howden. It's not difficult to envisage Andrew taking his elder sister up to Masham for an enjoyable outing. After all, it was as much a social event as a trading mart. It was also a place where there was stock to be valued and land and assets discussed: meat and drink to Willie. So it's not perhaps that much further a stretch of the imagination to think that Mary and William exchanged meaningful glances across a sheep pen.

Masham Sheep Fair 1905. Courtesy www.mashamhistory.com

As William's first wife, Sarah, had died in 1905, it's reasonable to think that a busy businessman was on the lookout for someone to look after his four children and help to run the day to day affairs of the house. Mary would seem to fit that bill admirably. As a farmer's daughter she knew how such a household worked. She was a good cook. She had helped with the running of her family's busy homes. She had spent some time looking after her parents, some 25 years older than her. Should an older gentleman wish for a housekeeper, Mary would seem an ideal candidate.

Possibly, what once began as a housekeeping role gradually evolved, causing romance to blossom. William's obituary, although written some 30 years later, perhaps summarizes the attraction, *"Willie' Hall, of the vigorous frame, twinkle in the eye, generous beard and ruddy complexion spelt Cumberland if anyone ever did. He was one of those men who gave dignity and honour to any calling"*. Did this man of many talents chance to meet the Blakeys in the course of his stock judging at Masham? And at such a meeting did his twinkling eye beguile a fair maid? Did he weigh up more than the quality of Andrew's flock? Who can ever know?

Whatever the cause, a relationship had clearly grown as Mary of Bowthorpe Hall and William of Evening Hill, Cockermouth were married in Howden in April 1909, a week after Mary's 33rd birthday. James was 55 - just 22 years older than Mary.

Life in Cumberland

The couple returned to Hall's house, 'Evening Hill', on the road to Brigham, to the south-west of Cockermouth. William had lived there since at least 1901. On the large-scale Ordnance Survey map of the area in the1890s a property of this name stands alone, in several acres of fields, close to allotments and the area of town known as 'The Moor' and is still in that state on the 1923 map.

Evening Hill House survives to this day, but is now surrounded by later developments, as presumably the farm land had been sold off. A neighbouring road on the estate is called Evening Hill Drive.

Evening Hill House in 2015. Courtesy of Cockermouth Heritage Group

Returning briefly to the 1901 census, in this William was described as *'farmer, shopkeeper and general draper'*, living in the 11-roomed property with 16 year old son, Thomas, a *'draper's apprentice'*; three daughters; first wife, Sarah, 82 year old mother-in-law, Hannah and 80 year old Uncle James, the man who brought William up as a child, who was described as *'retired farmer'*.

By the time of the 1911 census, Sarah, Hannah and Uncle James had died and Thomas had moved away. Residing at Evening Hill with William and Mary were Mary's three stepdaughters, Evelyn (28), Eleanor (18) and Mary (14), and a servant. William was now described as merely a farmer and draper.

In the latter role, Trade Directories show he had been a partner in Smails Brothers and Hall of 28 Main Street, Cockermouth for at least a decade. Whilst the company is no longer at this address, the property remains externally in much the state it was in William's time.

Smails, Bros., & Hall,

COCKERMOUTH.

Ladies' Hosiery, Corsets, Umbrellas, Blouses, Lace Goods, Skirts and Mantles of all kinds.

Household Draperies, Napery, Bedding and Furnishing Goods.

Gent.'s Hosiers, Hatters and Merchant Tailors.

Handbill for Smails Bros & Hall's business at 28 Main Street Cockermouth, circa 1910. Courtesy of Cockermouth Heritage Group

Life during wartime

Three years after the census, the outbreak of World War I caused huge social turmoil. Although Cumberland was a long way from the Western Front, the effects of the conflict rapidly reached the North West. The Red Cross understood that hospitals would need to be established to deal with those wounded at the front, and over 3000 so-called "auxiliary hospitals" were created across the country. One of the 27 in Cumberland opened at Cockermouth Castle.

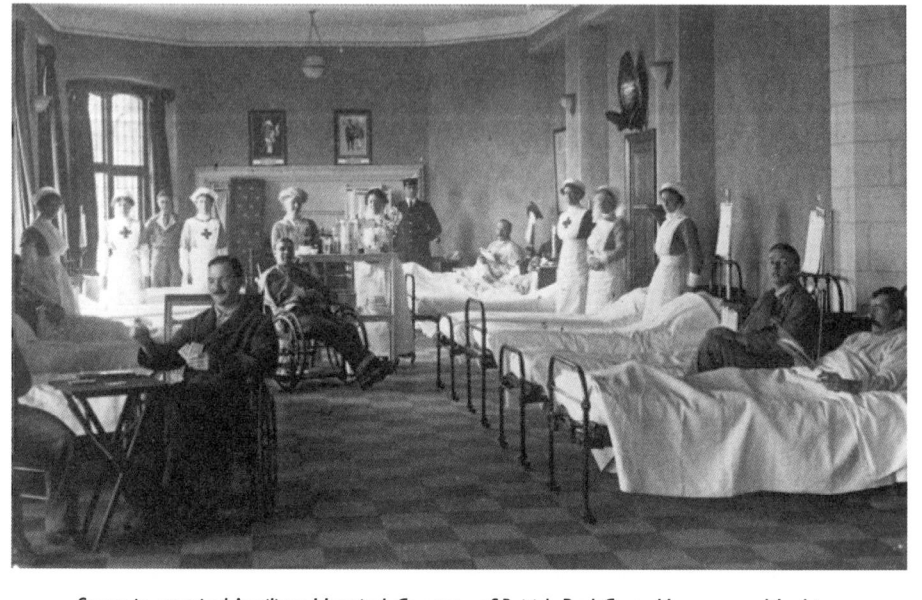

Scene in a typical Auxiliary Hospital. Courtesy of British Red Cross Museum and Archives

Records show that Mary volunteered to help with the war effort on 4th October 1914, almost as soon as hostilities had broken out, although the Cockermouth hospital is only recorded as opening in 1917.

The Red Cross reports that, "*In many cases, women in the local neighbourhood volunteered on a part-time basis. The hospitals often needed to supplement voluntary work with paid roles, such as cooks. Local medics also volunteered, despite the extra strain that the medical profession was under at that time.*

The patients at these hospitals were generally less seriously wounded than at other hospitals and they needed to convalesce. The servicemen preferred auxiliary hospitals to military ones because they were not so strict, less crowded and the surroundings were more homely".

Documents from Cumbria archives show that Mary was 'Commandant' of the hospital, effectively the senior non-medical person on site, responsible for all the administrative aspects of the running of the establishment.

The corps of voluntary nurses at Cockermouth. Courtesy of Cockermouth Heritage Group.

*Nurses and convalescing soldiers at Cockermouth circa1917. Reason for 'x' unknown.
Courtesy of Cockermouth Heritage Group.*

In both of these images it is possible that Mary is the central female character in the full nursing outfit, although that could be the Matron. This person does look similar to the woman on the extreme right of the wedding photograph later in this chapter.

She must have carried out her work in an exceptional way, as the 'London Gazette', the publication which lists all the Honours that have been awarded to citizens of the UK, announced in its issue of 26th March, 1920, the award of MBE to :

Mary Eleanor, Mrs. Hall.
Commandant, Cockermouth Castle Auxiliary Hospital, Cumberland

This award had been instituted in 1917 by King George V who wished to create an Order to honour many thousands of those who had served in a variety of non-combatant roles during World War 1.

After the war was over

Mary's life over the course of the next 15 years or so seems to have proceeded unremarkably, but it is surely impossible to think that a woman of such drive, talent and administrative skill, being married to a man of such agricultural renown would not have made important contributions to county life. Those tales will, however, have to remain in the pages of the local newspapers of the time. In terms of Mary's family life, the death of William's son in 1933 was the next crucial event, as it meant there was no male successor for William to hand on the farm and the business to. In turn it meant that, following the conditions in William's will, Mary's tenure at Evening Hill was likely to end on William's death.

Tantalising evidence of the link between Mary Hall and the Evening Hill property exists as a scrap of paper inside the cookbook. A roughly-scribbled recipe from a Mrs. Videll is on one side and the address, "Mrs. Hall, Evening Hill" on the other.

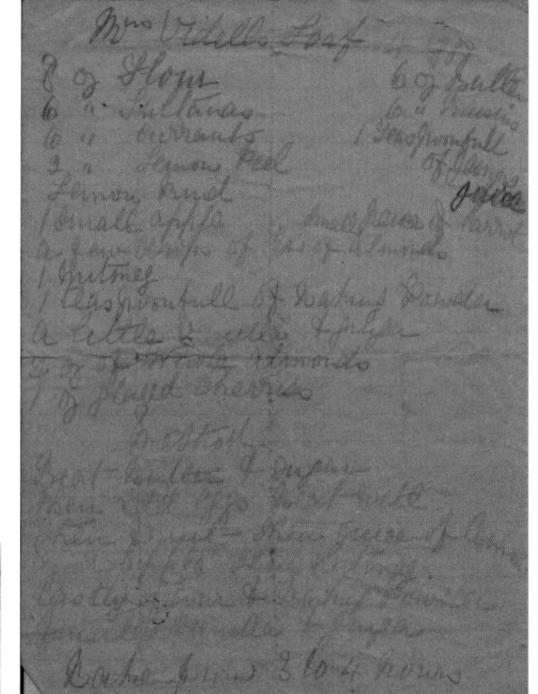

Was this recipe posted through the door of Evening Hill by Mrs. Videll? A neat version of the recipe is included at the end of chapter 5.

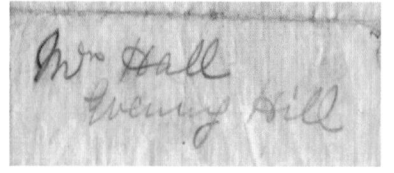

William's death

THE LATE MR. J. W HALL

REPRESENTATIVE FUNERAL AT COCKERMOUTH

The funeral of Mr. J. W. Hall, life-long partner in the firm of Messrs. Smails Bros. and Hall, Cockermouth, who died at his residence, Evening Hill, Cockermouth, on Wednesday, took place at Cockermouth Cemetery on Sunday and was one of the largest locally for some years. The Rev W Walton officiated. The cortege consisted of over sixty cars. Service was held in the Lorton Street Methodist Church.

The obituary and funeral notices printed in the local papers on his death in October 1937 show what a remarkable man Willie Hall must have been.

There is not space in a book about Mary to detail everything about her husband's life, but suffice to comment that the notices in the newspaper ran to over 20 column inches, his cortege consisted of over 60 cars and more than 100 mourners are listed, with floral tributes coming from as far away as Western Australia.

Whilst it is not certain, it seems probable that William was born out of wedlock in the small village of Bridekirk, north of Cockermouth and brought to Cockermouth to be raised by his mother's family and his uncle. From that position of disadvantage, he rose to be a master draper and important businessman in both Cockermouth and the counties beyond. He remained active in the drapery trade for over 60 years.

As well as this extraordinarily long stint in the clothing business, the obituary describes his Border Leicester sheep as "*renowned across the Borders*", as well as his being a breeder of champion Shorthorn Cattle.

He had attained high status in the Masons, being Past Provincial Grand Standard Bearer and latterly had been proudly appointed President of the Cockermouth Agricultural Society. He also was known for being a "*sound and reliable arbitrator*" and a valuer of farmsteads, land and stock. This skill was widely employed at agricultural shows across the North-West, and he was linked with Ireby Show for over 40 years. Politically he was described as a "*Liberal of the old school*".

He had also been responsible for setting up a charitable foundation to fund the Cockermouth's Pensioner's Christmas Treat, and as a young man he attended the Centennial celebrations of the USA in 1876.

The comments concerning his personality have already been referred to in the section of this biography concerning how William and Mary might have met.

In conclusion, William was described as *'one of the county's most prominent agriculturalists'*: surely a prime example of English understatement.

Willie Hall, as pictured in the 'Cumberland Times' of 23.10.1937 on the announcement of his death.

After William's death

William's will of 1910 names *"dear wife Mary Eleanor"*, his eldest daughter Evelyn, and a local banker as joint executors. Written in the first year of marriage, William made no changes to it over the next 27. He stipulated that, after the sale of all his real and personal estate, the residue upon trust is to pay an income to his wife (for as long as she remains his widow) and requires her to *"maintain a comfortable home for such of my children as shall remain unmarried"*.

He added, *"When the youngest child reaches the age of 21, the amount of capital and income is to be divided equally between his wife and all his surviving children."*

The proceeds of the sale amounted to £4 690 (about £200 000 today). By 1937, all three daughters were still alive and over 21, so the cash was split four ways. Mary therefore had around £1 200 (or £50 000 at today's values), but nowhere to live. She also had spinster stepdaughter Evelyn to take care of. Mary's life changed completely. This change happened rapidly. Between William's death in October 1937 and the proving of the will in January 1938, Mary had moved. The address on the probate forms is no longer Evening Hill, her home of 28 years, but a grander house still.

Her residence is given as 'Crackenthorpe Hall'. This lies just north of Appleby, 25 miles or so from Cockermouth, and in Westmoreland, not Cumberland. This is a very unexpected turn in Mary's life, with neither her Yorkshire nor Cockermouth families wanting to take her in after William's death. Stepdaughter Evelyn's arrangements remain unknown, but both she and sister Eleanor lived into the 1960s.

In 1938, Crackenthorpe Hall was owned by Leonard Cresswell JP. Cresswell was fully aware of the property's history and in 1932 had published a learned paper on the myths and history of the house, dating back to the 12th century, and that of the families who lived there, particularly the Machells. Cresswell had been a JP in the Burley area of Leeds, close to Mary's mother's home at Dunkirk. Could she have gone to live with a family friend from half a century ago? Or, as Mary was about to lose her home, and could not live for long on the capital she inherited, perhaps she either applied for a housekeeper's job or decided to pay rent at a suitable address.

Crackenthorpe Hall is set in 31 acres of gardens, grounds and woodland, with 1½ miles of river frontage. Noted visitors have included King Henry VI after his defeat by the Yorkists at Hexham in 1464, and King Edward VII when he attended the wedding of a son of the house, Percy Machell, to a great-niece of Edward's mother, Queen Victoria, in 1905. There may have been a Roman villa on the site, and the Hall has been the subject of Tudor, Georgian and Victorian alterations and additions. Pevsner, who chronicled notable buildings across England, mentions the Hall in his tour of Westmoreland. Today, Crackenthorpe Hall is undergoing renovation and is separated from its village by the A66, but remains a fine historic spot.

Frontage of Crackenthorpe Hall in 2008

23

Whatever her circumstances, sadly Mary's stay at Crackenthorpe was short-lived. Her death due to pulmonary thrombosis, following kidney problems, was recorded on 30th September 1939 at the Cumberland Infirmary, Carlisle.

Unsolved Mysteries

Rather than settling things, Mary's death leaves some teasing questions.

Despite the fact that William and Mary had been married for 28 years, Mary was not buried with William, nor is there any mention of her on his gravestone, although his first wife, two uncles and the deaths of his children are commemorated, with the final inscription being added in 1961. Why would his 'dear wife' not be there?

Another mystery is that, according to the Carlisle Bereavement Department, the details of her death have the name Eleanor crossed out. Was that to avoid a clash with the name of her youngest stepdaughter?

Finally, the 'informant' of her death is her sister Emily who had been living in Hemingbrough, rather than any of Mary's stepchildren with whom she had lived for 30 years.

Mary's gravestone in Carlisle

Mary lies entirely separately from any other Halls or Blakeys, in a gently-wooded and secluded part of the main cemetery in Carlisle. In death, the Blakeys were more generous to William's family than vice versa, mentioning she is the *"widow of J.W. Hall of Cockermouth"* on Mary's headstone. However, neither her MBE nor her service in World War I nor her wider families are referred to at all.

In contrast to the wide coverage of William's death, Mary's demise is merely recorded in five lines in the classified columns of the local paper.

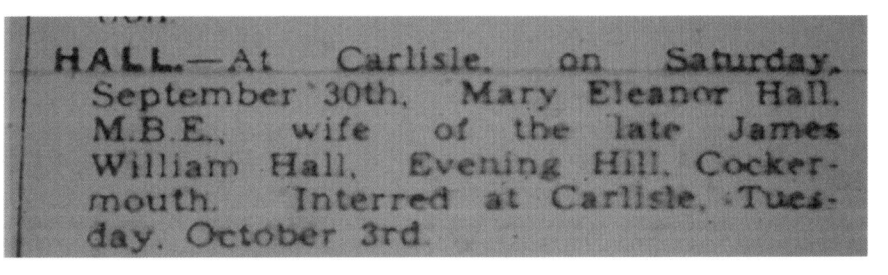

Details of the administration of Mary's estate

Mary's brother Andrew appears on the scene again, as he not only purchased the grave, but is also one of the administrators of her estate. In the two years following her husband's death, Mary's capital value had reduced by around £800 or two-thirds of the original sum. Was this rent for living at Crackenthorpe, or were the funds used to pay for her hospital treatment? The NHS did not come into being until 1948.

HALL Mary Eleanor of Crackenthorpe Hall Appleby **Westmorland** widow died 30 September 1939 at Cumberland Infirmary Carlisle Administration **Wakefield** 6 December to John Thomas Blakey and Andrew Hebden Blakey farmers. Effects £440 10s.

The administrators of the probate are listed as the Yorkshire-based Blakeys so Mary's effects at least did finally come back to the Broad Acres. It's reasonable to think that one of these was the cookbook.

How might the cookbook have come to a charity shop?

The journey of the cookbook from administration in Wakefield in 1939 to charity shop donation in Selby in 2012 is unknown. By far the most likely chain of events is that it returned with Mary's other effects from Carlisle, and passed through her brother Andrew's family. As descendents of the Blakey line still live at Bowthorpe, the book may have lain undisturbed in a forgotten corner until a clear-out and a trip to the charity shop brought it back to light.

For a book begun over a century ago, it remains in good condition. No pages are falling out, only one is ripped and the paper is not crumbling. It must have been in safe keeping during its 75-year long hibernation.

Are there any more clues about Mary's identity?

Perhaps Andrew has one further part to play. The three pages of 'other' notes in Mary's cookbook referred to at the start of this chapter mention Isaac Tyson of Hemingbrough in 1793 and details of relatives and descendents. Hemingbrough is about 5 miles south west of Bowthorpe.

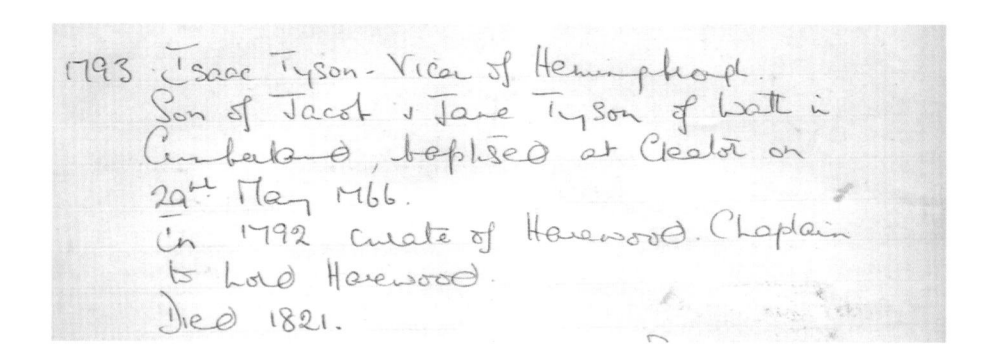

A sample of the 'modern' notes in Mary's book

As already noted, Andrew was well known for being a forthright man of action and with widespread agricultural interests. At the turn of the 20th century, the Tyson family were ironmongers and makers of agricultural implements of repute in Selby. The Blakeys and the Tysons clearly had reasons to do business with each other. Andrew also seems to have had romantic interests with a female member of the family, Gertrude, who was apparently known at the time as the 'Flower of Selby'.

The image below, is of the marriage party on the occasion of the wedding of Andrew Hebden Blakey to Gertrude Tyson. So, perhaps these 'other' notes are the work of someone researching Andrew and Gertrude's story? We can never know for sure, but it is a pleasing thought that Mary's book, which has brought on all this family history, should itself contain notes by someone else delving into other family roots.

Whatever the case, the happy couple are in pride of place at the centre of the front row of the picture taken around 1914. Family sources maintain that Mary is there, too. It is believed she is one of the ladies to the right on the back row. The woman on the extreme right does seem similar to the nurse at the centre of the Cockermouth picture taken a few years earlier.

The Blakey/Tyson wedding party at Bowthorpe circa 1914. Mary is possibly the woman at the extreme right-hand edge of the picture. Courtesy of the Blakey archive.

That is about as much detail as one can reasonably go into about Mary's life. Much of the detail of Mary's life as presented here is intelligent guess work. I must stress that I am not related (as far as I know!) in any way to either family, nor have any reason to wish them well or ill - and indeed I am grateful for information from the Blakey family in compiling this book.

Whilst William's will survives, the fact that Mary's effects are dealt with via administration means that Mary either did not write a will, or that any will was invalid for some reason. However, 75 years after the events, it is impossible to know which, so it is not possible to compare their final wishes.

lusion

vVhatever uncertainties arose after her death, Mary certainly lived a varied and fascinating life.

She grew up as a farmer's daughter in a Yorkshire hamlet, before living with famous neighbours in a farmhouse dating back to 1664. She then moved away from a tranquil countryside setting to the noisy hurly-burly of life in a busy industrial village, where, despite only being in her 20s, she planned and delivered a series of modern Domestic Science lessons and was an Assistant Mistress at school.

Mary returned to the family farming environment at another historic property before her marriage, a week after her 33rd birthday, took her away from her family across the Pennines to be the second wife of a farmer and businessman renowned throughout the Borders. A few years later she took a leading role in caring for wounded soldiers and was awarded an MBE for service to the country. Her demise came following what seems to have been a fall out with her family of 30 years standing, ending her days at one of England's oldest manor houses.

For at least 20 years in the middle of her life, she noted down over 150 recipes, along with her kitchen management tips, in that stout green notebook.

I'm really glad her marvellously-presented kitchen manual fell open on the way to the recycling bin. If it hadn't, then there would not have been the chance to bring Mary's wisdom to a wider audience nor to appreciate the twists and turns of her life.

I hope that you find my selection of her recipes and rules for a kitchen's regimen that follow as fascinating as I have done, and that you are encouraged to try some of them out.

Whilst further description of Mary's life may lie beyond the scope of a book that celebrates her description of Edwardian recipes and kitchen management, I have not given up my researches on Mary's life with the publication of this book.

Should anyone wish to contact me with corrections or additions, please do so via the details in chapter 8.

A list of the people and organizations who have kindly helped my quest, and publications referred to in researching Mary's life, are also in that chapter.

Mary's Evening Classes

We can't know for certain, but it is highly probable that Mary started her cookbook as an aid to the Evening Classes she taught in Rothwell. This was her syllabus:

> Syllabus for an Evening Class.
> (1) Must be attractive to the class of pupils for whom it is designed.
> (2) Scullery work must be taught, but it should be done in the middle or at the end of the lesson when its need is felt.
> (3) Frying is the favourite process of cookery among artisan classes, & often the only one possible on the fireplaces in their homes :. they usually have some practical experience of it, & in order to proceed from known to unknown, this syllabus begins with and makes frequent use of it.
> (4) Recapitulation must be had, but without monotony
> (5) As the taste and skill of the class increase, every opportunity must be taken of showing the value of variety in diet, and the means of making the most thrifty use of foodstuffs easily obtained in the neighbourhood of the class.

It is not difficult to imagine Mary striding from her lodgings up Commercial Street with a clear purpose as to whom she was going to instruct, and why that instruction was needed. As she puts it:

> Class. Factory Girls. Domestic Servants Lab'rs Daughte
> Aim (1) To teach the girls to cook well what they already like, and to increase their manual skill, variety of diet; & interest in common food stuffs (2) To teach cleanliness, thrift & consider ation for others

This syllabus was very advanced for her day because Mary tried to build upon what her students already knew, rather than preach at her girls. This point is developed in more detail in chapter 7. Here are her first ten lessons:

I   Fried Steak & onions   Rules for Shallow Frying & for
    Jam Tarts   Pastry Making.
    S.W. How to Clean Frying-pan
    Tartlet tins
    Pastry Board.

II   Fried Bacon & Bread.   Choice, prep. & boiling of potatoes
    Mashed Potatoes. Scones   S.W. Cleaning of pastry board, knives.
    Recap of I

III   Sausage Pie. Spotted Dick   Precautions nec. with regard to
    sausages. Rules for making
    Suet Pudd. S.W. Earthware dishes
    & iron saucepans.

IV   Cheese Pudd.   Value & use of cheese with some
    Fried Potatoes.   warnings.
    S.W. Cleaning white metal & Recap of.

V   Smoked Haddock   Value of fish as a food
    Apple Turnovers   S.W. Cleaning of oven, & baking shal.

VI   Pea Soup. Fried Bread.   Rules for soup making   Steel
    Baked) Plum Pudd.   Value of soup. S.W. Recap Saucep.

VII   Irish Stew. Pancakes.   Rules for stewing. Cleaning Stewpan

VIII   Savoury meat & potato   Rules " Cold meat Cookery
    pie. Rice Pudd.   S.W. Rem. stains & charred food
    from pie dishes. Cl. Plated goods.

IX   Boiled Bacon Pease Pudd.   Rules for boiling Value of pulse
    as a food

X   Bread. Grilled Kippers   Rules for Bread Making with
    on Mashed Potatoes.   Yeast.

Mary is trying to gradually increase the level of her students' skills whilst attempting to create interesting meals on a strict budget. The meals also had to give the 'man of the house' the energy needed to keep at a physical job. This is also discussed in more detail in chapter 7.

Before looking at her recipes, consider how Mary might have amassed such knowledge of kitchen skills. The answer seems to be the age-old one of learning at your mother's side.

Mary was the eldest daughter of the family, and so would have been the first in line to learn kitchen skills. Mary's mother, Sarah, had been brought up in an isolated farmhouse in the hamlet of Dunkirk, in Wharfedale, above Ilkley. In such circumstances, one had to learn to make the best of all supplies, and family sources maintain that Sarah was quite a cook.

It's a fair guess then that Mary learnt her skills watching and helping her mother in the kitchens at Clint, Hincks Hall and Howden. As mentioned in the previous chapter, Dunkirk is also close to Burley, which may have been an important factor at the end of Mary's life, at Crackenthorpe Hall.

The twenty-something Mary who began the book in 1903 may have been young in years, but with an old head on young shoulders. As a contemporary kitchen management book put it :

"A cook must know her pots and the item she is making. She has no thermometer to tell how hot her fire is, nor does she have a recipe that calls for a '350 degree oven.'Time is the best teacher and many a young cook, learning at her mother's feet, came close to ruining a meal. Since one could ill afford to toss something out, rest assured, mom was very watchful. She would likely let the novice get just to the edge of the point of no return before stepping in to set things right."

Mary's aim was to be able to "increase skill, improve variety of diet and interest in common food...with thrift and consideration for others."

Personally, I think she achieved this wonderfully. I hope as you read some of her recipes, you'll think so too

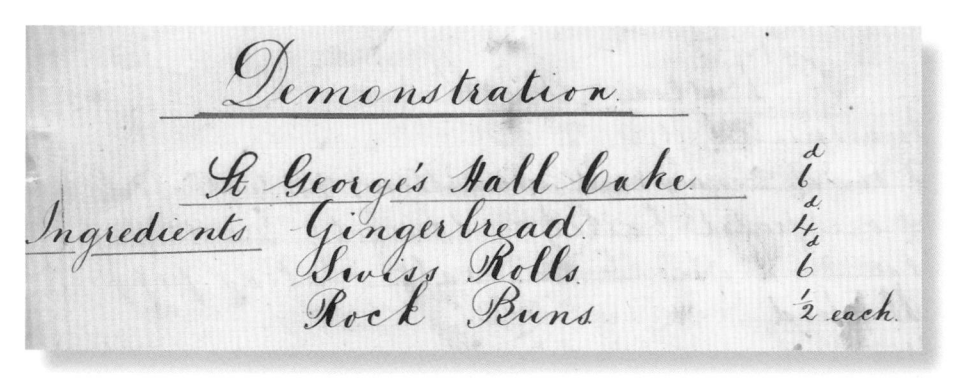

Here are Mary's final nine lessons. As the school year is traditionally 40 weeks long, Mary's lessons might have been fortnightly.

XI	Roast Mutton & Potatoes Gravy. Boiled Cabbage.	Rules for roasting. " " boiling green veg. Sw. Cl. dripp-pan, skewers, & saucepan.
XII	Stewed Tripe & Onions. Bread & jam fritters.	Sw. Cl. stew pan & frying pan.
XIII	Fried Liver & Bacon Steamed apple Dumpling	Rules for steaming contrasted with R. for frying. Cl. wooden tables & boards.
XIV	Stuffed Potatoes with Gravy. Baked Batter Pudd.	Rules for Batter making. Value of potatoes in cookery and cleaning. Cl. steel & tin utensils
XV	Fish in batter. Fruit Tart.	Choice & cleaning of dish Rules for making Rough Puff Pastry. Sw. Cleaning glass & china.
XVI	Stewed Shin of Beef with Dumplings. Cake.	Rules for choice of Meat " " Cake making.
XVI	Macaroni Cheese. Boiled Plum Pudd Sweet Sauce	Rules for Sauce making. Value of Sauces. Cl. earthenware vessels & enamelled saucepans.
XVII	Italian Fish. Little Cornfl. Blanc manges.	Cleaning glass removing stains Hints on choice of Shell fish
XIX	Exetorstew Forcemeat Balls Gingerbread	Rules for Cake making Use of Salt. vinegar & soda in cleaning

Artisan Cookery

This stylish heading atop the first page of Mary's recipes, sets the tone. An artisan is defined as a skilled craft worker who makes or creates things by hand. Mary intends her students to gain culinary skills to produce nutritious meals.

In her Evening Classes syllabus, Mary is keen that students *"make the most thrifty use of foodstuffs easily obtained from the neighbourhood of the class"*. Given that most neighbourhoods would have had a butcher, baker and greengrocer, and a visiting fishmonger, Mary expects her students to use these suppliers to advantage, along with produce available from Rothwell's market gardens. The supply of food in 1903 is discussed in chapter 7.

The selection of recipes that follow include some from her lessons and others that she noted in her book. They begin with basics such as pastry and sauces, and move on to main courses with meat and vegetables. Cakes and puddings are considered in the next chapter.

These recipes may seem a million miles away from the low-fat, health-conscious meals of today, following the latest fads and trends. But in many ways, Mary was equally meeting the needs of her time. Men did heavy manual work, and so a diet rich in fat provided the energy store they needed. With money being short, thrifty use of every part of even the cheapest ingredients was essential.

We might worry today about the level of fat, and therefore cholesterol in the meals that Mary suggests. The normal span of life was much shorter a century ago, and concern about the diseases of the blood system that excess cholesterol might cause in later life, if they were thought of at all, were very much a secondary concern to ensuring that manual workers had sufficient food in their bellies to do their job.

Mary's syllabus states that she wants to *"proceed from the known to the unknown,"* a sentiment that would fit well in modern syllabuses. Specifically, she plans to make her students progress from frying on the fireplace where her students *"have some experience"* to long, slow cooking by steaming over the hob or in the oven of the kitchen range. Mary was also quite up-to-date in her choice of recipes. Whilst meals such as stews had been a staple dish for centuries, some of her other recipes were first seen in cookery and household management books of the preceding decades. Quotes from these accompany some of Mary's recipes.

Main meals, Sauces, Vegetables

Short Pastry and Suet Crust

Making good pastry was vital for savoury and sweet pies, and essential to achieve Mary's goal of weaning away students from the frying pan. There are several kinds of pastry and Mary gives instructions for three kinds that will see her students well provided for in most situations.

When Mary was growing up, the most common form of fat used in pastry was lard. The kind of margarine we know today as 'hard' margarine' was invented in 1869 and came into common use thereafter. Butter could be used for a richer pastry, and sugar could be added for sweet pastry creations.

Lard is rendered pig fat, a cheaper ingredient than butter, but with a higher fat content. Short pastry is used for the base of a tart, pie or quiche. Suet, being specifically the fat around a cow or sheep's kidneys, might have come from the butchers' rather than a packet.

Short Pastry.

4 ozs. flour 2ozs. lard ¼ teas. B.P. Salt.
cold water.

Method.

Mix B.P. and salt with the flour. Now rub in the lard. Mix to a stiff paste with cold water. roll out twice, and it is ready.

Suet Crust.

6 ozs flour, 3 ozs. suet finely chopped. ½ teasp: B.P.
Salt. Cold water.

Method.

Mix flour, suet salt & baking powder together Mix to a stiff paste with cold water. Roll out on a floured board in a round piece & use at once.

Flaky Pastry

'Flaky' refers to the small flakes of fat that expand as the pastry is cooked, forming the layers that make eating apple turnovers or sausage rolls so enjoyable. Incorporating these flakes calls for more skill than straightforward shortcrust. Although Mary says the recipe is without butter, she refers to it in her method, and also makes a little error, as circled.

> _Flaky Pastry (without butter)_
> 4 ozs flour. 2 ozs firm lard. ¼ teasp: Salt
> Cold water.
>
> _Method._
> Divide the lard in three portions, and rub one into the flour. Add the salt. Mix to an elastic dough with the water. Now roll out & place the second lot of lard on in small flakes, dredge with flour, fold in three, turn with open edge of pastry to & from you, roll out Put the rest of the butter on in same way, flour fold, roll out. (Put the rest of the) and put away for at least 1 hr. in a cold place. Roll out twice more, & it is ready to cut to shapes required.

Baking Powder

B.P. was first formulated by Alfred Bird of custard fame in 1843. This is Mary's recipe.

> _Baking 'Powder._
> 7 ozs rice flour. 6 ozs Carb: of Soda. 4 ozs Tartaric Acid
> _Method_
> Have all these things very dry, & mix them well together - pass through a fine sieve or strainer, & be careful to get out all the lumps. Put into a bottle and keep it airtight.

Bread

Although bread might be thought of as a staple in the diet, Mary does not demonstrate it until her 10th lesson. Perhaps she considers that her students do not, until that time, have the necessary skill to deal with the living organisms in yeast.

Once Mary has introduced the idea of yeast cookery, she goes on to deal with yeasted buns, tea cakes and cakes.

7. *Demonstration*

Bread	Small Quantity.
3½ lbs flour.	1 lb. flour.
1 oz yeast.	½ oz yeast.
1 tablesp: salt.	1 teas: salt.
About 1¾ pts. luke warm water.	About ½ pt. lukewarm water.

Method

Place the flour in a warmed bowl. Add 1 teas. sugar to the yeast, and mix till liquid, add one teacup of warm water to it, now pour it into the middle of the flour, and let it rise 15 minutes.

Sprinkle salt round the edges, and knead it up with as much luke warm water, as will make rather a stiff dough; knead well until quite smooth, let it rise 1 hr.

Make into loaves, place in a warm greased tin and rise before the fire about 20 mins. Bake in a quick oven from 50 mins to 1 hr. according to the size of the loaf.

Yorkshire Pudding, Gravy, Mint Sauce

Any Yorkshire lass worth her salt had to be able to make a good Yorkshire Pudding to go with a nice bit of meat for the Sunday roast. Here's Mary's method. A 'quick' oven is presumably a very hot one to cook the batter quickly, avoiding a soggy pudding.

> ### Yorkshire Pudding.
> 4 ozs Flour, ½ pt milk. 2 teas: salt. 1 egg. A little clean dripping
> Beat the egg add the milk to it, and stir very smoothly into the flour. Add salt and let it stand ½ an hour. Make the dripping hot in a tin, pour the batter into it, and bake in a quick oven for about ½ hr. Cut into squares, dish on a hot dish and the pudding is ready.

A good Yorkshire benefits from some lubrication, like gravy, or, if you were lucky enough to have some lamb, then mint sauce. Mint grows very easily in the meanest kitchen garden. Mary's 'browning' is caramelised brown sugar dissolved in water.

> ### Gravy.
> 2 oz butter. ½ oz flour. ½ pt stock. A little gravy browning, and seasoning.
> Melt the butter in a pan, add the flour and cook a few minutes. Now add the stock gradually. Bring to a boil, stirring all the time, cook well, add browning and seasoning and gravy is ready.

> ### Mint Sauce
> Pick the leaves from the sprigs of mint wash, dry and chop very finely. Add 3 or 4 tablesp: vinegar and ½ tablesp: fine white sugar. Stir to dissolve the sugar & the sauce is ready

Main Meals

Whenever possible, the idea was to have some kind of meat in the main meal of the day. A roast joint on the Sabbath, if the budget ran to it, or cheaper cuts stewed slowly. The cold cuts could be used during the week, either as they were or minced into pies, rissoles or cutlets.

Irish Stew

According to the Oxford Companion to Food, Irish Stew is a "*celebrated Irish dish. Purists maintain that the only acceptable and traditional ingredients are neck of mutton chops, potatoes, onions, and water.*" Mary's recipe marks her out as a purist. Ideally suited to cooking on the range as it required long, slow cooking, with not much in the way of observation apart from a stir now and again and the occasional skimming off of any fat.

Irish Stew.

1 lb neck of mutton or scraps. 1½ lbs. potatoes
1 onion   ¾pt water.   Salt. Pepper. Flour.

Method

Cut the meat into chops, trim if necessary. dip each in flour. Place in a pan. Peel & slice the onion on the top. Season. Add the water & bring to a boil. Wash, peel & slice the potato put them on the top of the meat, & let it all simmer for two hrs.
Add more water or a little bone stock if necessary when the potatoes are quite soft & the meat tender, dish up, with the meat in the centre & the potatoes round.
If trouble is no object the stew is nicer with the potatoes half cooked before being added to it. In this case give the meat ¾ hr. before & ¾ after adding the potatoes.

Toad in a (or the) Hole

This is effectively a development of the Yorkshire Pudding/batter recipe.

Mary sticks closely to the advice given by Charles Francatelli in 'A Plain Cookery Book for the Working Classes' (1861) where he emphasizes the dishes' thrifty origins by specifying *"bits and pieces of any kind of meat, which are to be had cheapest at night when the day's sale is over."* It's not that long ago when butchers and bakers used to sell items at cost price if they wouldn't be palatable the next day. The Oxford English Dictionary's first recorded example of *"toad in the hole"* isn't until 1787, though references to a dish that sounds similar can be found somewhat earlier.

Hannah Glasse - a cook of Northumbrian origin - mentions *"Pigeon in a hole"* in her 1747 book 'The Art of Cookery Made Plain and Easy'. The young birds or squabs were readily sourced from pigeon cotes. A Georgian shopkeeper, Thomas Turner, notes a dinner of *"sausages baked in a batter pudding"* in his diary of 1757. In Isabella Beeton's well-known Victorian 'Book of Household Management', the meat specified is chuck steak, which seems a little extravagant, but not as extravagant as Pippa Middleton who advised the use of Parma ham in 2013.

Toad in a hole.

2 ozs. flour. ¼ pt. milk. ½ egg ¼ teasp: B. Powder Salt. 1 link of sausage or scraps of cold meat.

Method.

Beat the egg, and add the milk to it. Mix it with the flour smoothly, beating the whole time. Let it stand ½ hr.

Make a teasp: of dripping hot in a pie-dish. Add B. P. and salt to batter. Put the sausage freed from skin, and divide in small pieces into the piedish. Pour the batter over, and bake in a quick oven until batter has well risen, and the sausage cooked through.

Shepherd's Pie

Purists would specify mutton, but any leftover or scraps of meat can be used.

Today we tend to make this from fresh mince, but in Mary's time, minced cooked meat was more usual, giving a totally different texture. According to Mrs. Beeton, the pie dish was to be lined with mashed potato as well as having a mashed potato crust on top.

The term 'Shepherd's Pie' did not appear until 1877, the idea being that Shepherd's Pie referred to a meal like this being made with lamb or mutton as shepherds dealt with sheep. Cottage Pie was an earlier invention, implying a poor man's meal given the large amount of potato - seen as a pauper's food - used in the recipe.

Shepherd's Pie.

Full quantity	Small quantity
½ lb scraps of cold meat	2 ozs scraps of cold meat.
1 small onion (½ boiled)	¼ small onion (½ boiled)
½ teacup stock	2 or 3 tablesp: stock
½ teasp: salt.	Pinch of salt.
¼ " pepper	" " pepper.
1½ lbs. cooked potatoes	6 ozs cooked potatoes

Method
Chop the meat and onion finely, add the gravy and seasoning
Mash the potatoes - add a little warm milk and salt, and beat well.
Lay the meat in a greased pie dish, pile the potatoes on the top, make it rough with a for. and put a small piece of butter on the top
Bake for about ½ to ¾ of hour until the top is nicely browned.

Today, 'Cottage Pie' and 'Shepherd's Pie' are often understood to be effectively the same dish, regardless of meat used.

Boiled Ham, Roast Pork

Mary provided recipes to do justice to good cuts of meat, too. Whilst boiling can cook any reasonable joint of ham, the Good Housekeeping Cookbook describes Pork Loin as an 'expensive but prime cut'.

Boiled Ham

4 lbs of ham.
Soak the meat all night in cold water. Then scrape it and just cover with cold water, bring to a boil, and cook very gently, allowing about ½ an hour to each lb. and half an hour over. Now remove ham, and peel off all the outer rind. Sift over it some browned and pounded bread crumbs, and the ham is ready.

Roast or Baked Pork

Take about 2 lbs of loin of pork, and score the skin in strips about 4" apart. See that the loin is jointed. Make some dripping hot in a tin, place the meat in it. Place in a quick oven at first then in a cooler part, so as to cook the meat through. Baste occasionally.
Allow ½ to every lb & ½ hr. over.
Dish up the pork.
Strain away the fat from the tin, leaving the brown sediment, which is the gravy. Pour in about ½ pt. of boiling water, add salt, strain in a pan, bring to a boil and skim. Pour round the joint. Sprinkle the joint with a little dried and sifted sage.
Serve with sage and onions and apple sauce in separate sauceboats.

Meat Pies

Once they had learnt pastry skills, Mary's students were expected to use them in making a lid for a veal and ham pie, and both base and lid for the beef steak. In Dickens' 'Pickwick Papers' (1836-7), a character mentions *"beef-steak a kidney"* pies, using ingredients from Sweeney Todd. Perhaps not the most palatable of delicacies.

Veal & Ham Pie

2 lbs. lean veal   Salt & pepper to taste
½ lb. ham   Stock or water to ½ fill dish
2 hard boiled eggs   A good flaky crust

Cut the veal into pieces about 1½" long by 1" wide. Cut the ham also in strips & remove most of fat. Half fill a piedish with the cut up meat & ham. Sprinkle in salt & pepper, then put on rest of meat & season again. Cut the eggs into four & lay on top. Half fill the dish with stock or water. cover with a crust, brush over with egg. decorate & brush again with egg. Put in a quick oven at first till pastry is well risen, then lower the heat. giving the pie altogether about 1½h

Beef Steak Pudding.

1½ lbs. of Beefsteak   Salt. Pepper. Flour
¼ of a beast's kidney   Suet crust.

Method.
Cut the steak in thin slices, place in a small piece of fat on each, roll up and dip in flour.
Line a well greased basin with suet crust. Put in the steak, and the kidney cut into small pieces, season each layer. Half fill the basin with cold water. Wet the edges put on a lid of pastry. Cover with greased paper and steam 3 hrs.

43

Durham Cutlets

According to the 'Foods of England' website, the earliest record of this recipe is, surprisingly, from Wales in 1880. The macaroni is inserted to imitate a bone in an attempt to fool the diner into thinking this is a real cutlet off a joint! This dish is a good example of a meal using leftovers from the Sunday joint, as referred to earlier.

+ **Durham Cutlets.**
¼ lb cooked meat. ½ small onion (half cooked)
1 oz flour. 1 oz butter. ¼ pt stock, salt, pepper,
and cayenne, egg and bread crumbs, and
small pieces of macaroni.
Method.
Chop the meat and onion finely. Melt the
butter in a pan, add the flour, and gradually
the stock. Cook well, add the meat and
onion to it, and season. Spread on a
plate to cool. When cool, cut into pieces,
and form each piece into a cutlet. Dip in
egg, toss in bread crumbs, and fry in hot
fat, till a pale brown. Drain on soft paper
put a small piece of macaroni into each
and dish up in a circle.

Why the dish is called Durham Cutlet is unclear. There are several recipes in Mary's book (not all featured in this book) that have names linked to places. Some have no clear connection : "Brazilian" and "Lancaster Stew" seem little different from their Irish cousin but "London Buns", (not Chelsea), described in chapter 5 hail from New London, Connecticut. Mentioned by Be-Ro in 1904, they are also known, for no clear reason, as 'London Johnny Boy'.

As later references to curry powders and pastes, as well as the specification here for cayenne pepper, show, Mary's students were expected to have access to a range of condiments beyond just salt and pepper.

Curry

People may think that curry is a relatively new addition to the British palate. Those of a certain age may remember the joys of Vesta boil-in-the-bag meals of the 1960s and 70s. This recipe shows that currying as a way of using up leftovers was alive and well in Yorkshire a good half century before that.

What is unusual is the addition of rhubarb to the mixture. However, as Rothwell is and was part of the famous 'rhubarb triangle' perhaps cooks were encouraged to use it wherever possible. Certainly the principles of long, slow cooking to make a good curry are evident here. She also suggests squeezing lemon juice on the curry when serving the meal with rice. Mrs Beeton describes 'curry butter' which is a mixture of that fat, curry powder and lemon juice. Mary's rice recipe is on page 59.

Curry of cold meat.

Ingredients.

Any scraps of cold meat ½ to ¾ lb. 1 onion 1 oz butter. 1 tablesp: of grated cocoanut. ½ pt. stock. ½ oz rice flour or ground rice. 1 tablesp: of curry powder and curry paste mixed. A small sour apple, or 3 or 4 ins of rhubarb to take place of apple. A little tomato to improve flavour, salt.

Method.

Pour the stock on to the cocoanut, let it stand for a short time. Mince the onion finely, fry it in the butter, now add the stock strained, the rhubarb or apple minced, the curry powder, paste, and rice all mixed together with a little cold water. Add salt, stir until it boils. Now place the lid on the pan, and cook the sauce gently from ¾ to 1 hr. Then place in it the meat cut into small pieces, and cook the curry for about ¾ hr

She does not have any recipes for poppadoms or onion bhajis.

Hashed Mutton and Potato Border

A hash was a third way of making a tasty meal from leftovers. Here it's mutton, but the same principles could be applied to beef or pork. 'Hash' derives from the French verb 'hacher' meaning to chop, and refers to the fact that to make this meal you have to chop everything up. The most well-known modern version is corned beef hash, often now served as a breakfast rather than a main meal.

Mary suggests that her hash is served with a potato border. When you look at how she treats other vegetables, this method of preparing the spud conserves many more of the nutrients than her 'boil them to death' instructions for carrots, sprouts and cabbage.

Hashed Mutton

Some slices of cold mutton. About ½ pt of stock flavoured with onion. ½ tablesp: of flour. Salt, pepper, and some small pieces of fried or toasted bread.

Trim the meat carefully from all pieces of gristle or fat. Chop up the bones, place in a pan, and just cover with cold water. Add an onion, and simmer about 2hrs. to make the stock. Strain off the stock into a pan, add the slices of meat, cook gently about ¾ to 1hr. Mix the flour with a little cold water, stir into the gravy, add salt and pepper, and cook about ½ hr. longer. Now dish up the meat, and put the pieces of fried bread round.

Potato Border.

About 1 lb of potatoes after peeling, some hot milk, salt and pepper. Steam potatoes, dry well, mash with a fork, or put through a masher. Add a little hot milk to them, beat well, put on to a hot dish and make into a border.

Rissole, Liver and Bacon

Another use of leftovers; rissoles used to be available in West Riding chippies.

> **Rissoles of cold Meat**
> ¼ lb of cooked meat   2 small onion, half boiled
> ¼ oz of very finely chopped suet   1 oz bread crumbs
> About 2 tablesp: of stock or gravy   1 heap of
> chopped parsley   Salt and pepper
> **Method.**   Breadcrumbs and egg for coating
> Chop the meat very finely, soak the bread
> in the stock. Mix meat and crumbs together
> Now add suet, parsley, and finely chopped onion
> season, add more stock if necessary, Make up
> into small balls, dip in beaten egg, and then roll
> in bread crumbs, and fry in a deep pan of
> hot fat. Serve with a nicely thickened gravy.

Often offal was the cheapest form of red meat available. This is a basic use of her students' favoured cooking method of frying.

> **Fried Liver & Bacon.**
> 1 lb Calves or Sheeps Liver   2 tablesp: flour
> 1½ oz Dripping   ½ lb bacon
> ¾ pt warm water
> **Method.**
> Slice the liver, sprinkle with flour, & fry in the
> dripping quickly. Place in a stew jar or pan-pour
> the fat away, add ¾ pt warm water - pour
> over the liver & let it all simmer ½ an hr.
> Mix the flour with cold water-stir into the gravy
> let it boil, cook well, season, dish up the
> liver in the centre of the dish, & put fried bacon
> round.

Tripe

Even cheaper than offal was heart, tripe, chitterlings, and the like. Tripe is basically the intestine of cows or sheep. Similar fare from a pig is called chitterlings. Although Mrs Beeton calls tripe a *"connoisseur's food"*, to make this offal edible it has to be cooked for a very long time, and even then, any flavour is mainly due to the vegetables and stock it is cooked in.

Tripe and onions was a northern favourite. In 1906, Manchester had over 250 tripe stalls, and Wigan had a "Tripe de Luxe" restaurant seating 300. Such days are long gone, but tripe stalls remain in markets in places like Bury and Barnsley. Tripe-based dishes remain popular in continental Europe, being low in calories, high in protein and a source of trace minerals.

Stewed Tripe.

1 lb. tripe.   ¾ pt milk.   1 sm. tablesp. flour. 2 onions
Salt   Pepper.

Method

Wash the tripe, cut in pieces that can easily be served. Place in a pan on an old plate. Add milk, peeled and cut up onion. Simmer about 1 hr. Strain off the onion. Chop it up finely. Mix the flour with cold water, pour the hot milk on to it, return to pan. Stir until it boils. Now add the onion. When hot replace the tripe in it, and when hot it is ready.

Tripe in Batter

½ lb tripe. Frying batter. Fat.
If the tripe seems tough, stew it ½ hr. in milk and water. Now cut into pieces about 3" square. Dip in batter and fry in hot fat. Drain & dish up, serving with onion sauce.

Even the Bard has a phrase : in by-play in 'Taming of the Shrew' he has Grumio asking Katherine *"How say you to a fat tripe, finely boiled?"* The reference may be more innuendo than in your kitchen, but it does show that folk have been eating (and possibly speaking) tripe for centuries.

Stuffed Sheep's Heart

Some may still eat tripe, but do people still eat sheep's heart? It is a very cheap and wholesome food, being rich, red-muscle meat, although the preparation as described here is not for the squeamish! I am told that heart is still available in the meat section of certain supermarkets.

Since the fat linked to meat is responsible for much of the flavour, and heart muscle has very little fat attached to it, a herby stuffing is necessary to enhance the flavour.

Stuffed Sheeps' Heart

2 sheeps hearts.
2 ozs bread crumbs.
1 oz suet (chopped)
½ tablesp: chopped Parsley.
¼ teas. dried Thyme.

1 small egg.
Salt. Pepper.
1 oz dripping.
¾ pt. stock
½ tablesp: flour

Method.

Wash the hearts and cut away the pipes. Squeeze out all the blood

Mix the crumbs, herbs, suet & seasoning together & bind with the beaten egg.

Fill the hearts with the stuffing (do not press it at all) tie a piece of strong greased paper over each and fry quickly in the hot dripping - pour away the fat, add the stock made hot, & simmer gently 2 hrs

Mix the flour with a little cold water, pour some of the gravy on to it - boil up, add salt, & dish up the hearts removing paper. Pour the gravy round.

NB They may be plainly roasted if liked.

Boiled Rabbit

Rabbit has been a very popular food in England for centuries. Grand houses and religious foundations would have their 'Warriner' - the man who attended to the rabbits in their warrens to provide a cheap source of white meat. The surname 'Warren' is thought to derive from this.

For the poorer folk, rabbits were classic poachers' fare and there are many apocryphal tales of branch-line steam loco drivers exchanging coal from the tender for a pair of freshly-caught bunnies.

Rabbit remained popular until the 1950s, being gradually replaced by chicken as a source of white meat. Recently it has made somewhat of a comeback in 'proper' butchers' shops. However, even they aren't 'proper' enough to expect you to skin the beast and deal with the head!

Boiled Rabbit

Skin, draw & wash the rabbit wipe it. Take the head, & bring it round so that it lies against the forelegs. Bring the back legs forward, & the fore legs backwards towards them, & skewer them together, tie with string. Place in a pan of boiling water to which you have added enough salt to slightly taste it. Bring to a boil & simmer gently about 1hr. Serve with onion or white sauce poured over it.

Rabbit meat was once commonly sold in parts of Sydney, Australia, so much so that the local rugby league team became known as the South Sydney Rabbitohs. The meat became unpopular once the disease myxomatosis was introduced to try to eliminate feral rabbits.

Stocks, Soups and Broths

These warming and nourishing fluids were another staple item of the diet, especially in winter. Stocks were the simplest formulation, made by lengthy boiling of a carcass with vegetables and herbs to add flavour. Stocks were rarely served on their own, but formed the base for a broth or soup. If times were really hard, water substituted for stock. Generally speaking, broths were simpler than soup, normally derived from the cheapest cuts of meat. Mary's Sheep's Head Broth utilizes the cheapest of the cheap. Scotch Broth with added barley was an exception to the rule. The term 'soup' implies that more processes had gone on to produce the final meal. The stock cube we all know and love today was first produced by Oxo in 1910, just too late for Mary's lessons.

Mutton Broth

Mutton is the meat of an adult sheep. It is tougher but has a stronger flavour than lamb, so needs slower cooking. A broth, hotpot or casserole are therefore ideal methods. 'Scrag end' means the upper part of the neck of the beast, part of the anatomy known to those humans who get into a fight, grab the neck of their assailant, and so are said to have 'scragged' their opponents.

Bone Stock

A bag of bones could be had for virtually no cost from a butcher, and the marrow inside the bone was full of goodness. But what a procedure to have to get at it! Chopping up bones, cleaning, skimming and stewing for nine or more hours : not only hard work, but one dares not think of the smell that must have filled the house.

After all that, the liquid has to be cooled and sieved, too. The resulting broth was indeed good for you : an excellent source of minerals and known to boost the immune system and improve digestion. Its high calcium, magnesium, and phosphorus content make it great for bone and tooth health. Bone broth also supports joints, hair, skin, and nails due to its high collagen content. The old wives saying that recommended a dose of chicken soup to cure many illnesses is probably based on the goodness extracted from the marrow in the bones.

Concerns about BSE and CJD mean it's probably impossible to buy loose meat bones to follow Mary's guidance today, and unwise even if you could.

Bone Stock.

Chop up the bones well, wipe them, and put them in a deep pan.
Cover well with _cold_ water; bring to a boil, skim, & put on the pan lid.
Simmer all very gently for 9 or 10 hrs.
Plenty of water may be used to allow for waste in the long stewing.
If the water is hard, add 1 tablesp: brown sugar to it.
When the stock is done, strain through a hair sieve, and it can be used for anything for which stock is required.

Sheep's Head Broth

Broths were made from the cheapest cuts of meat, but even for the least squeamish, the preparation of this dish can't have been the pleasantest of tasks.

Tongue remains a popular sandwich meat, but modern health considerations rule out the use of brain in food served to humans.

Sheep's Head Broth

1 Sheep's head	3 qts. cold water.
1 or 2 carrots.	1 turnip
2 or 3 onions	3 potatoes
3 pieces celery	4 leaves of sage.
2 tablesp: oatmeal	½ teacup of Rice or
Salt and pepper.	Pearl barley.

Method

Wash the head with salt and cold water remove the nose bones. lay in cold water for an hour (remove the brains first & soak them) Tie the brains up in muslin and sage leaves) Place head in a pan with given quantity of water, bring to a boil and skim. Cut the vegetables into small dice, add to the pan with rice or barley. (soaked) Season and simmer for 3 hrs. When the soup has simmered two hrs. add the brains, and also oatmeal previously mixed with a little cold water Now remove the head and carefully take off all the meat

Skin and split the tongue, arrange it on a small dish, chop up the brains, add salt & pepper, put them on the split tongue. Serve this with parsley sauce.

Pea Soup

Peas here are split peas rather than the green garden ones common today. These peas were dry, hard and perfect for naughty children to use in pea shooters. Culinary use required overnight soaking or 'steeping' to make them palatable. Sometimes the peas were supplied with special steeping tablets made of sodium bicarbonate that softened the pea's skin to allow it to absorb water more easily.

This recipe is an example of where the goodness extracted in bone stock was used to increase the nutritional value of a basic soup. The pea mixture could also be made into more solid fare like pease pudding, well-known for accompanying faggots. As the nursery rhyme has it, in that form it will last for a long time, but might need a bit of spicing to make it palatable!

Pease pudding hot, Pease pudding cold, Pease pudding in the pot, Nine days old!

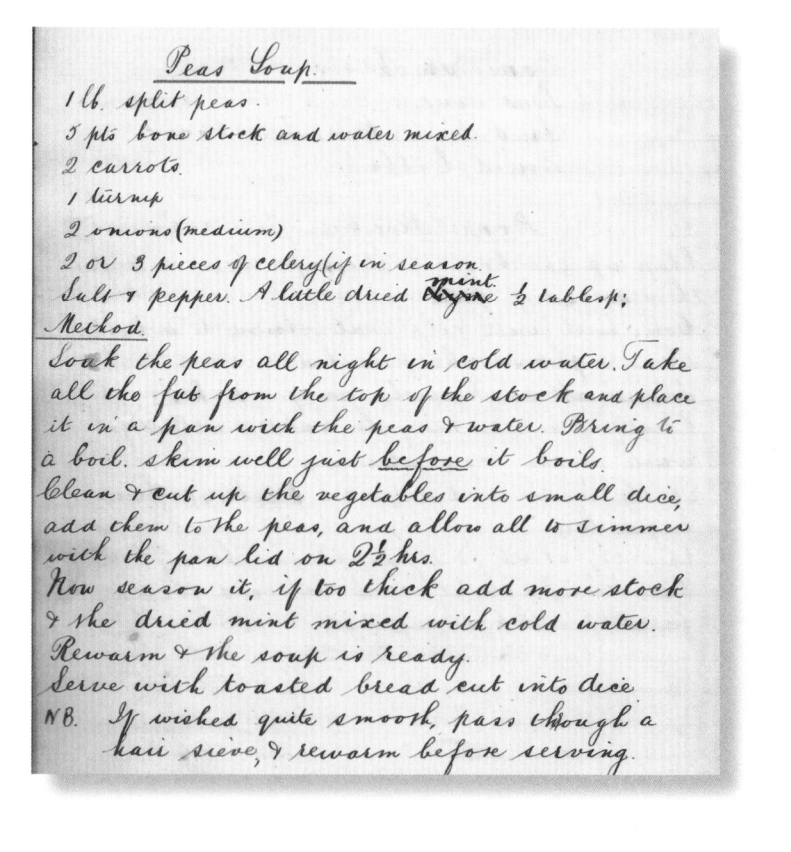

Fish

Fish and chips became popular in England in the middle of the 19th century. Dickens mentions a *"fried fish warehouse"* in Oliver Twist, and in the North of England a fashion for deep-fried chipped potatoes developed. The first chip shop was in Oldham, and a Mr. Lees seems to have combined the two ideas of fried fish and chipped spuds in Mossley in 1863.

As fresh fish was becoming more readily available inland due to the spread of the railways carrying catches inland from the ports, Mary gives recipes for several types of fish. However, quite what is the 'Italian fish', referred to in lesson 18 in chapter 3, remains unclear.

Fried Sole

1 lemon sole, salt and lemon juice, egg, crumbs, and fat for frying

Method.

Skin and fillet the sole, cutting each fillet in two pieces. Sprinkle with salt and lemon juice, dip in beaten egg and crumbs. Make some dripping smoking hot, putting in the pieces of fish, and fry a nice brown. Drain on soft paper. Dish on a hot dish garnish with parsley, and serve with any suitable sauce.

Anchovy Sauce.

¾ oz of butter, ¾ oz flour, ½ pt milk or milk and fish stock mixed. 1 teas. anchovy essence. Salt & pepper.

Method

Melt the butter in a pan, add the flour, and cook a few mins. Now add the liquid gradually. Bring to a boil, stirring all the time, cook well add the essence & seasoning & sauce is ready.

Baked Stuffed Haddock and Brown Sauce

Mary's fishmonger hasn't prepared the fish to the degree that we might expect today. Doubling the tail back through the eye sockets is a little like the way that roll mop herrings are presented today - but the weight of fish here is somewhat greater. Mary's Brown Sauce is less fruity than our modern versions. You might use Mary's browning, as mentioned earlier in her recipe for gravy, or purchase commercial 'Browning', a blend of caramel colour, vegetable concentrates and seasonings, first on sale around the turn of the 20th century.

Baked Stuffed Haddock.

1 Haddock 2½ to 3 lbs in weight.
3 ozs old bread (crusts)
1½ " finely chopped suet.
2 tablesp: finely " parsley
½ Teasp: dried Thym
3 Tables: milk
Little cold water
½ teas. salt
¼ " pepper.

Method

Clean scrape and trim the fish. Take out the eyes wash and wipe it. Soak the bread in the milk and water until soft. Drain all the liquid from it, and beat it up quite fine with a fork. Add the suet, herbs, and seasoning, and stuff the inside of the fish with it. Sew or skewer it up. Put the tail through the eyeholes, fasten with a skewer. Make 2 ozs of dripping hot in a tin, put in the haddock, dredge with flour, & bake. Allow about ¼ hr. to each lb. Baste well. Dish up and serve with brown Sauce.

Brown Sauce.

½ oz butter. 1 Tables: flour. ½ pt. fish stock or water. Salt.
2 tablesp: vinegar. A few drops of browning.
Melt butter in a pan, add flour, then gradually the water, stir until it boils. Cook well. Pour away any fat from the tin, pour the sauce in the tin, Add vinegar, if needed more browning & salt. Strain & it is ready.

Vegetables

It does seem strange that whilst Mary takes great care to get every ounce of nutrition out of meat and fish, the length of time that she suggests you cook vegetables removes any vestige of goodness. No wonder children had to be forced to eat up their greens! However, Mary is suggesting that the roots are boiled whole rather than ringed, sliced or diced as we might do today. The sweetness of carrots is known in carrot cake, but it is odd to see sugar added to a boiling mixture. The addition of soda is meant to keep the colour in the sprouts. The turnip is presumably the Yorkshire purple-topped white-fleshed variety rather than the Scots' yellow root.

Boiled Carrots

Brush and wash the carrots- scrape & throw into cold water, have ready a pan of boiling water, add ½ tablesp: salt to each quart of water & 1 teasp: sugar. Put in the carrots, & boil till tender 1 hr, or over. drain, cut in pieces and serve.

NB. If very thick, split in half before boiling

Boiled Turnip

Peel the turnips, throw into cold water. Have ready a pan of boiling water, add ½ tablesp: salt to each quart of water & 1 teas. sugar. Boil till tender 45 mins or more. Drain, cut in pieces and serve.

Boiled Sprouts

Wash the sprouts in salt and water. Trim off some of the outer leaves & throw into cold water. Have ready a pan of boiling water, add salt to taste & a little Carb: of Soda. Boil for 15 to 20 mins. drain well & dry near the fire. Dish up & they are ready.

Boiled Cabbage

Wash the cabbage well, first removing the outer leaves, and all discoloured parts. Cut in half & remove some of the thick stalk, & let lie in cold water with salt. Now plunge into a pan of boiling water, to which has been added salt to taste, ½ teas. of carb: of Soda. Boil with pan lid off for ¾ hr. or till tender. Drain & squeeze well in a colander. Chop. add salt & pepper & teas. of butter. Now put in hot dish, & cut across with knife.

To her credit, Mary alleviates the texture of her vegetables by suggesting a variety of sauces to go with them, or with other dishes she recommends.

Boiled Asparagus

Cut off some of the white stalks of the asparagus, scrape slightly the white part left, let it lie in cold water. tie in bundles. Have ready slightly salted, boiling water, and a teasp: of sugar. Boil the asparagus for about 20 mins, or until the heads are tender. Be careful not to break the heads at all. Drain. Serve if liked on toast. Stand butter melted and clarified round with the asparagus or Hollandaise Sauce or oil and vinegar.

Melted Butter for Asparagus

2 ozs of butter.
Just make hot in a pan, skim off the froth, pour the clear oily part off into a hot sauceboat, add a few drops of lemon juice if liked and serve quite hot.

Boiled Spanish Onions.

Peel the onions, throw them into a pan of boiling water, to which has been added salt enough to taste. (½ tablesp: to a quart) Boil for 1½ to 2 hrs. according to size of onion A very large one would require longer Drain and serve with white sauce.

White Sauce.

¾ oz. flour, ¾ oz butter ½ pt. milk. salt. Melt the butter in a pan, add flour, mix well, stir the milk gradually in. Bring to a boil, cook well, add salt, & it is ready

Boiled Rice

Patna rice is named after the capital of the Indian state of Bihar. As most long-grained rice sold in England at the time came from Bihar, 'Patna' was the name given to any good quality long-grained rice.

Boiled Rice

4 lb of Patna rice.
Plenty of boiling water a little salt.

__Method__

Bring the water to a boil, add the salt, stir in the rice, and boil with the pan lid off from 15 to 18 mins. Now drain on a wire sieve using a fork, if it requires turning. Rub out the pan with a little butter, put back the rice in it. cover with a clean cloth, and put it by the fire until required.

Colcannon

Colcannon was originally an Irish dish of autumn and winter when that hardiest of green vegetables, kale, was widely available. Using the most basic of ingredients, it nevertheless produces hearty and filling fare. Mary's recipe misses out the milk or cream normally used to enrich the mixture, and substitutes cabbage for kale.

Just as in Christmas Pudding, small coins could be hidden in the cooked dish - possibly as an encouragement for young 'uns to eat it up!

To really make a meal, this might be served with the boiled ham mentioned earlier (page 42).

The first verse of a song in honour of the dish runs:

Did you ever eat Colcannon, made from lovely pickled cream?
With the greens and scallions mingled like a picture in a dream.
Did you ever make a hole on top to hold the melting flake
Of the creamy, flavoured butter that your mother used to make?

Colcannon.

½ lb cooked cabbage
½ ,,   ,,   potatoes
2oz butter or clean dripping
½ onion half boiled
Salt. Pepper. Bread crumbs.

Method

Grease a basin well & then sprinkle with the crumbs. Chop the onion & chop the cabbage. Mash the potatoes & mix well together then stir in the butter (melted) & seasoning, & press the mixture into the prepared basin. Put into a quick oven for about 45 mins
Turn out into a hot vegetable dish.

Puddings and Cakes

As noted in the introduction, in keeping with a thrifty approach to kitchen management, the puddings Mary prepares for classes generally use the most basic of ingredients. However, Mary's complete cookbook describes many more recipes than she taught her students, some of which call for more complicated techniques and more expensive ingredients. What follows is a selection from the entire spectrum, with a few notes about the history behind some of the recipes.

Pancakes

In the introduction to her syllabus, Mary expresses concern that her students only know about using the frying pan. So, before she goes on to describe cakes made by steaming or baking, or the use of pastry to make tarts, she describes a simple batter recipe for pancakes. She is very down to earth : no tossing of pancakes, just gentle turning.

Pancakes

¼ lb. flour.   2 ozs flour.
1 or 2 eggs.   1 egg.
½ pt. milk   ¼ pt. milk
½ sm: teasp: salt.   ¼ sm. teasp: salt

Method.

Beat the eggs well, and beat them into the flour, adding the milk slowly - being careful that there are no lumps. Let it stand ½ hr.
Make as much dripping hot in a pan (frying) as will grease the bottom of it. Put in as much of the mixture as will cover the bottom of the pan. When brown on one side, turn and brown the other. Turn out on to a hot plate. Sprinkle with lemon juice and sugar. Roll up & sift sugar over it. Serve at once.

According to tradition, pancake racing started in Olney, Bucks in 1445. In that year, when the church bell rang out calling villagers to service, a virtuous local housewife was still at her stove. busily using up her stocks of fat and flour before Lent by preparing pancakes. Not having the time to stop to put down her pan, she ran to church, still in apron and headscarf, urgently tossing her pancake to prevent it from burning.

Amused locals thought this a scene worth repeating, so organized pancake-tossing races in following years.
These still go on to this day, with the housewives, in full pinny and mop cap racing to church and then attending the Shriving service.

Avon Cakes

A simple scone-type recipe. Mary's recipe for Baking Powder is listed in the pastry section.

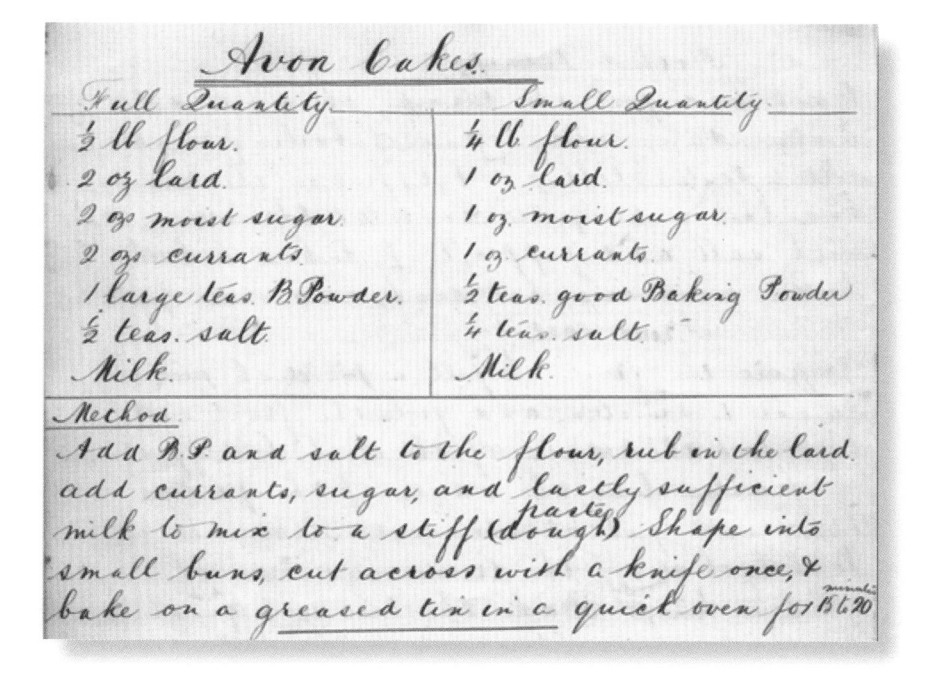

63

Teacakes

Similar to the scones, but a slightly increased level of difficulty with the use of yeast. Tea cakes are a tea-time basic. Easy to make, easy to toast on the fire, with a bit of butter or fat added to lubricate, and, of course, a mug of tea. Mary refers to a 'quick' oven again, as she did in her recipe for Yorkshire Pudding.

Teacakes.

2 lbs. flour	1 lb. flour
1 oz yeast	½ oz. yeast
4 ozs sugar	2 ozs sugar
4 ozs currants	2 ozs currants
4 ozs lard.	2 ozs. lard.
2 teasp: salt	1 teasp: salt
Luke warm milk	Luke warm milk

Method

Add 1 teasp: sugar to the yeast, and mix till liquid, add 1 teacup of warm water to it

Place the flour in a warmed bowl, rub in the lard, pour into a hole in the centre, add a little warm milk if necessary - let it rise about 15 mins, then knead up with the rest of the milk into a light dough, until it does not stick to your hands. Now let it rise 1 hr.

Knead in the currants and sugar, & when it has stood a short time (20 mins) make up into small cakes. (the whole quantity makes 10) roll them flat, & place on a greased tin, allow to rise about 20 mts: bake in a quick oven from 12 to 15 mins.

Rock Buns, Sultana Cake

Then, as now, Rock Buns are a simple first cake for beginners to bake. Mary makes a rare mention of costs in her rock bun recipe : 12 buns at ½d each, so it wouldn't be too disastrous if a learner chef did a King Alfred.

If a cook could afford it, butter would have been a better choice. As Mrs Beaton puts it, "*Good fresh butter, used in moderation, is easily digested; it is softening, nutritious and fattening, and is far more easily digested*

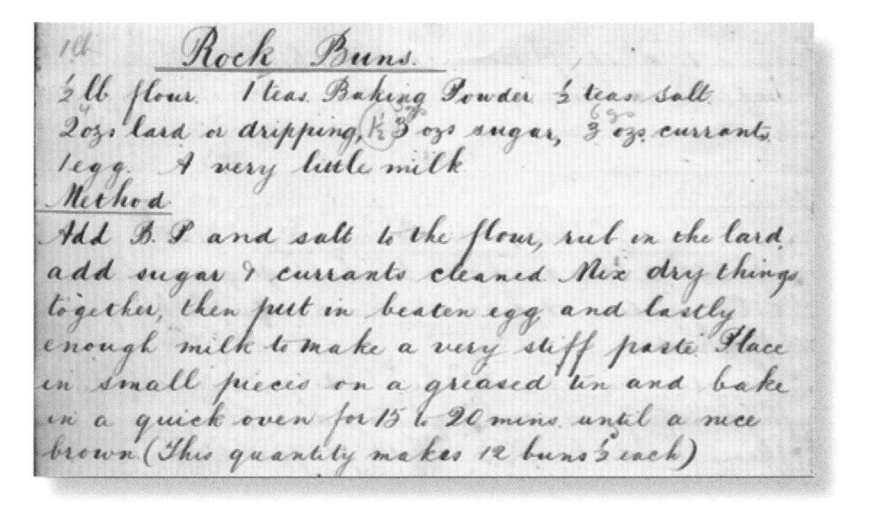

The Sultana Cake recipe gave a slab cake rather than buns, from similar ingredients

London Buns

These buns are a version of the Bath Bun. Florence White in her 1932 book "Good Things in England" updates a recipe used at the Great Exhibition of 1851 in London. White was writing several years after Mary, so Mary must either have known the original, or have seen the American source mentioned on page 44. The buns are best eaten very fresh, split in half with a nice spread of butter.

The taste and texture is reminiscent of that celebrated confection, the Fat Rascal, made famous by a Harrogate bakery, which is not that far from Mary's roots. It would be easy to add more dried fruit for an even closer approximation.

London Buns

1 lb flour	½ lb. flour	¼ lb. flour
4 ozs lard	2½ lard	1 oz lard
6 ozs sugar	3 oz sugar	1½ ozs sugar
2 teasp: Baking Powder	1 teasp B.P.	½ teas: Baking Powder
1 or 2 eggs	1 egg	½ an egg
1 teasp: salt	Salt	Pinch of salt
¼ pt. milk	⅛ pt milk	1 tablesp: milk
1 teas. ess. of lemon		A few drops of ess. of
or 2 ozs candid peel		lemon or ¼ oz candid peel
Some crystallized sugar		Some crystallized sugar

Method

Add the B.P. & salt to the flour, rub in the lard. Now add the sugar, flavouring beaten egg & milk.
Place in small pieces on a greased tin sprinkle coarse crystallised sugar on the top, & bake in a quick oven for about 20 mins.
The full quantity makes 20 ½ buns.

Scrap Bread Pudding

Not to be confused with bread and butter pudding, this is an excellent example of Mary's thrift in using up stale bread by cooking it with dried fruit, spices and cheap fat.

A pudding made from such basic materials would be of use in times of shortages. The Women's Voluntary Services for Civil Defence understood this and published a similar recipe in 1940 in a pamphlet called *'Communal Feeding in Wartime'*. In this it had quantities *"to feed 100"*. Mary may have seen it in Francis Underwood's 1890 book *"Cookery for Working Men's Wives"* or just learned it at mother Sarah's side.

Scrap Bread Pudding

Full Quantity
- 2 lb scraps of bread
- 3 ozs suet, finely chopped.
- 3 ozs currants
- 2 ozs sugar.
- 1 egg
- ¼ pt milk.
- Salt. Nutmeg

½ quantity
- ¼ lb scraps of bread
- 1½ ozs suet
- 1½ . currants.
- 1 . sugar
- ½ egg.
- ½ a ¼pt. milk.
- Salt. Nutmeg.

Method

Soak the crusts in cold water until soft, drain all the water away and drain with a plate as dry as possible. Beat with a fork. Next add the suet. currants (cleaned) Salt sugar, grated nutmeg, beaten egg, & lastly the milk. Turn into a greased basin cover with a greased paper & steam for 1½ hrs. The same pudding may be baked & if so, then a little more milk may be added. Serve with melted butter.

Spiced cakes using nutmeg, caraway and pepper, as well as ginger, have local variations throughout the country. A well-known Yorkshire variant is parkin, with added oatmeal. This was traditionally made around Bonfire Night. Mary was aware of a lesser-known version, which produced a gingery cross between a cake and a biscuit.

This was "Moggy", an East Riding recipe perhaps linked to Beverley, fairly close to where Mary's family went to farm.

Moggy

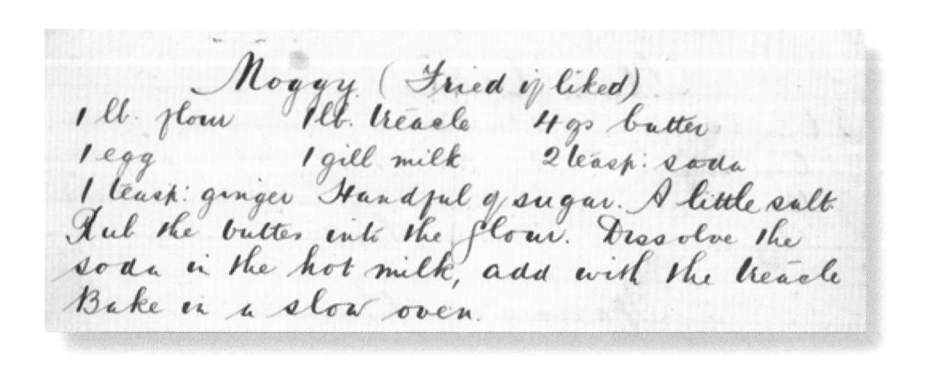

The name has nothing to do with the culinary quality of cats, but rather is said to derive from the Norse 'mugi' meaning 'a pile of grain''. Moggy is one of the last recipes that Mary records in her book. It is a little lacking in detail, and the amount of milk and cooking time is unspecified. It seems to work with just sufficient milk to dissolve the soda and make a smooth mix with the 'treacle', and then baking until the cake is just gently browned.

'A Taste of Britain' describes Moggy as a very sticky form of parkin, particular to the North of England. The 'Yorkshire Magazine' of 1871 mentions Moggy as "*a cake made of parts of flour, meal, potatoes and fat*". It advises that it should be eaten with "*lashings of custard*".

The thought of frying a piece of ginger cake, as suggested next to the title, seems odd in the extreme. Correspondent Dorothy Woodall remembered Moggy being made at home from a 1930's Women's Institute recipe. '*It was intended as a cheap and filling cake. We always had it buttered*'. As with most spiced cakes, the flavour improves if the cake is left for a few days in an airtight tin, or is securely wrapped.

Gingerbread Pudding

Puddings could also be steamed as well as being cooked in the oven. Steamed puddings played to the slow-cooking strengths of the kitchen range, as they needed little attention whilst cooking, provided the boiling water was kept topped up. Both spicy and fruity versions were popular.

Plum Pudding

A steamed, fruity pudding has been part of English cookery since medieval times. Mary's plum pudding contains no actual plums, as 'plum' in Victorian times had become a culinary term for raisins. This kind of pudding is still well-known today as Christmas Pudding, traditionally made on "Stir-up Sunday", the week before Advent, when all members of the family take a turn in stirring the mixture and making a wish. This reference has a spiritual link, too.

The 'Book of Common Prayer' lists this Biblical quote for the Sunday before Advent:

"Stir up, we beseech thee, O Lord, the wills of thy faithful people; that they, plenteously bringing forth the fruit of good works, may by thee be plenteously rewarded".

Mary refers to using a greased basin to cook her puddings, but steamed puddings really came to the fore in the 17th century when the pudding cloth was first used, replacing earlier vessels such as the stomach linings of a cow.

Plain Plum Pudding.

Small Quantity	Large Quantity
2½ ozs bread crumbs.	5 ozs bread crumbs.
3½ " flour	7 " flour.
2 " suet	¼ lb suet
2 " raisins	¼ " raisins
2 " currants.	¼ " currants
1 " moist sugar.	2 ozs moist sugar
½ teasp. Baking Powder.	1 teasp. B.P.
½ small teasp mixed spice	1 sm. teasp. mixed spice
1 egg	2 eggs
Nearly ¼ pt milk	Nearly ½ pt milk.

Method.

Chop the suet finely, add it to the flour, with the bread crumbs, sugar, and B.P. Put in the currants cleaned, and raisins stoned. Mix well together, add the well beaten eggs and milk. When well mixed turn into a greased basin, cover with greased paper, and steam 3 hrs.

The link between Plum Puddings and Christmas may stem from a pamphlet called 'Christmas Entertainments', dating from 1740. The Plum Pudding season was usually autumn, when dried fruit became available. A different kind of availability was apparently sought by Casanova, in pursuit of an English maid. He believed a typically English pudding would win the day and ordered his Italian chef to make a Plum Pudding. History does not record the outcome!

Black Cap Pudding

This combines both a batter mix, as in pancakes, and the steaming techniques used in plum puddings. The recipe is a traditional Irish one, originally using a fruit that now is very rare, black raspberries. A similar effect can be obtained by using fresh blackcurrants instead, although more sugar would be needed to overcome the currants' tartness. Here Mary goes for the even easier option of dried currants.

Black Cap Pudding

Large Quantity	Small Quantity
5 ozs flour	2½ ozs flour.
¾ pt milk	¼ pt. x 2 tablesp: milk
2 eggs	1 egg.
1½ ozs sugar.	¾ oz. sugar.
¼ teas. salt.	Pinch of salt
A few currants	A few currants.

Beat the egg, & add the milk to it, stir this smoothly into the flour. Add salt & sugar, & let it stand for ½ hr. Now well butter a basin, sprinkle currants on the bottom of it, pour the batter into it, cover with greased paper & steam for 2 hrs. Turn out and serve with melted butter sweetened.

In Eliza Acton's 'Modern Cookery for Private Families' of 1845, when referring to Black Cap pudding, the advice is: *"All batter puddings should be despatched quickly to table when they are once ready to serve, as they speedily become heavy if allowed to wait".*

All of the puddings mentioned to date would benefit from 'proper' egg custard to accompany them. Mary, of course, has a recipe.

Proper Plain Custard

Mary's recipe is for 'proper' custard made by heating and mixing cornflour, milk and egg. This may be a little more time-consuming and require more care than the now-familiar sweet yellow sauce that Alfred Bird invented in 1837, but is more authentic, and probably tastier.

> ## Plain Custard
>
> ½ pt milk   1 whole egg
> 1 teasp: cornflour   1 oz sugar.
> ### Method
> Mix the cornflour with a little of the milk. Make the rest warm with the sugar in it. Now pour it on the cornflour, return to the pan, stir until it boils. Take off, pour on to the beaten egg, & stir over the fire until the egg is cooked. The custard must not boil after the egg is cooked or it will crack.

Mrs Bird was apparently terribly allergic to eggs, so husband Alfred developed and patented a mixture of cornflour, vanilla essence and colourings so that his wife could fully enjoy her pudding. Alfred has a memorial in Key Hill cemetery, Birmingham. Bird's Custard Powder was made in the city until 1964, and the Custard Factory site is now an art, music, theatre and business complex.

BIRD'S CUSTARD POWDER produces exquisite Custard without eggs. The unfailing resource of every successful Hostess when catering for large or small parties.
BIRD'S CUSTARD,—Rich and Delicious with Plum Puddings. The one thing needed with all Stewed, Bottled, or Tinned Fruits.
NO EGGS!   NO RISK!   NO TROUBLE!
☞ **THE FESTIVE SEASON.**—A Dish of BIRD'S CUSTARD with any kind of Fruit is always received with acclamation at Children's Parties.

73

Apple Dumplings, Bird's Nest Pudding

Fresh fruit was another healthy and cheap ingredient for puddings. Sago was a starchy food from Indonesia that came in small grains, slowly cooked in milk, a bit like rice pudding or semolina. If sago was not to your taste, apples could also be baked in pastry and the dumplings set in custard.

Apple Dumplings.

Short Pastry (4 ozs flour, 2 ozs lard. Salt. B.P. Sugar Large apples.

Peel & core the apples without cutting them open. Roll out the pastry, cut into rounds put the apple in the centre of each piece fill up the centre with sugar, wet round the edge of the pastry, punch it up on the top of the apple. Place it on a greased tin (invert the apple) brush over with cold water, dust over with white granulated sugar, bake in a quick oven, until the apple is tender, & the pastry cooked.

Bird's Nest Pudding.

3 ozs. Medium Sago	1½ oz. medium sago.
1½ pts cold water	½ pint cold water
4 good sized apples.	2 good sized apples.
Sugar to taste	Sugar to taste.

Soak the sago in the water for 1 hr, then place in a pan, bring to a boil, and simmer until the sago is quite clear. Sweeten the sago. Peel and core the apples without cutting them open. Place them in a greased pie dish, fill each hollow with sugar. Pour the sago when clear on to the apple, and bake in the oven until the apples are quite tender.
NB Sago must be thin enough to easily pour into the dish

Mrs. Parson's Stir up Rhubarb pudd

Mary began her book in 1903, whilst living in Rothwell, at the heart of what is now deemed the 'rhubarb triangle'.

This area of the West Riding, was, at the time, bounded by Leeds, Wakefield and Bradford. It has moist soil and a frosty microclimate, ideal for 'forced' rhubarb which was successfully introduced to the area in 1877,

The scarlet winter shoots, botanically speaking a vegetable not a fruit, provided fare for tasty puddings around the start of a New Year, a time of year when fresh produce was scarce.

The forcing process involves rhubarb roots, or 'crowns', being kept in sheds in total darkness, and so forced to bring forth slender, sugary, red shoots, using energy stored in the roots from previous summers' growth.

Rhubarb Road Sign at Carlton near Rothwell

Rhubarb growing produced valuable income as well as providing a staple food. The forced variety was seen as something of a luxury commodity. Until 1966, from January to March, 'rhubarb expresses' delivered up to 200 tons of crop from the triangle to the markets of Covent Garden and Paris and exclusive emporia such as 'Harrods'. As well as London, produce was distributed wholesale to Birmingham, Leicester, Cardiff, Liverpool, Manchester, Newcastle, Glasgow and Southampton. This economic success, along with the plant's hardy and prolific nature, meant rhubarb was widely available locally in both forced and summer forms.

Correspondent Angela Swann reports that although the trade had declined, in 1967, over 500 acres was still given over to rhubarb in the Rothwell area. In the three winter months, around 6 000 tons was produced.

Forcing rhubarb in cold, squat, pitch-black sheds was back-breaking and time-consuming work. Whilst it occupied a monopoly position in the availability of 'fruit' early in the year, the effort was worth it for the price that the crop commanded away from the West Riding. However, the stems were not so valued in the Broad Acres.

But, sadly, rail distribution failed, more exotic fruit became more widely available and the palates of the post-war generation turned to less tart tastes. As small producers, who grew little else, gave up and retired, the business was left to the bigger farms.

Some thought rhubarb had the strength to stick up for itself, but gradually the trade wilted, as year-round competition from these less strident-tasting fruits increased. However, many still grew rhubarb in their gardens, for personal consumption in summer as "green top".

Nowadays, Wakefield, Morley and Rothwell are considered the vertices of the 'triangle'. Forcing sheds are still to be seen in the area and some growers offer tours of their sheds. Wakefield holds an annual rhubarb festival in February.

Mrs. Parson's Recipe

Rhubarb is traditionally made into jams, stewed up with custard or forms the base for a crumble. As Mary was not local, the idea of forced rhubarb was probably a novel experience. It's to her credit that she is willing to give something new a try and borrows a recipe from a Mrs. Parson. This incorporates the stems into a mixture for a pleasantly-stodgy steamed pudding.

Mr Parson's Recipe.
Stir up Rhubarb Pudd.
1½ lbs rhubarb (cut small)   1 egg
10 oz flour   ½ oz. baking powder
3 oz suet   Pinch of Salt
One quart sized basin.
Mix with milk or water, not too soft, but
fairly firm.
Stir all together & boil 2 hrs.

Preserving fruit

It might not have been possible to make use of a glut of fruit all at once. Mary's students had no freezers to turn to, but fruit could be bottled. Mary's bottling technique was comprehensive - but oddly made no specific reference to Kilner jars, which had been made in the West Riding since the 1840s.

> ## Bottling Fruit.
> Heat the jars in boiling water (put into cold water and bring to a boil, then pack them nearly up to the top with fruit, previously picked over & wiped Pour quite boiling water over, so as to quite cover, then pour a layer of paraffin wax on the top and tie down with strong paper brushed over with white of egg. Keep in a cool dry cupboard

Which fruit to use? Apricots and peaches are perhaps unexpected items, but gages, damsons and gooseberries were common allotment or hedgerow fare.

> ## Notes.
> Fruit should be sound and fresh
> "   "   " gathered on a dry day
> Kinds of fruit to bottle
> Green gooseberries. Damsons. Greengages.
> Apricots. Peaches
> In each case
> 1 Heat kills the germs.
> 2 Air excluded
> Oil, lard, suet, paraffin wax

Potato Cheesecake

This is perhaps the most unlikely recipe in Mary's book. Potato Cheesecake really does use common spuds, not the more exotic sweet potato. It is indeed a cheesecake without cheese and seems to derive from Lincolnshire-based celebrations of a successful harvest. It is a sweet, not savoury, dish. The taste is more reminiscent of a curd tart with potato being a substitute for curd.

Potato Cheesecakes.

Full Quantity	Small Quantity.
6 ozs cooked potatoes	2½ ozs cooked potatoes
4 " sugar	¾ ozs sugar
1½ " butter	½ " butter
3 " currants	¾ " currants
Rind & juice of ½ a lemon	Rind & juice of ¼ lemon
or 1 oz finely chopped	or ½ oz (sm) candid Peel
Candid Peel.	finely chopped.
1 egg	½ egg

Method.

Mash the potatoes, beat the egg. Melt the butter - mix all the ingredients together, grating in the lemon rind & straining in the juice. Mix all well together.

Line small tins with pastry - put some of the mixture into each, & bake in a quick oven for about 20 mins.

For the small quantity use 3 ozs flour & 1½ ozs lard. for the short pastry.

Fancier Desserts

Mary knew everyday cooking could produce somewhat more exciting items. The next few recipes show some of her more elaborate cakes.

Swiss Rolls

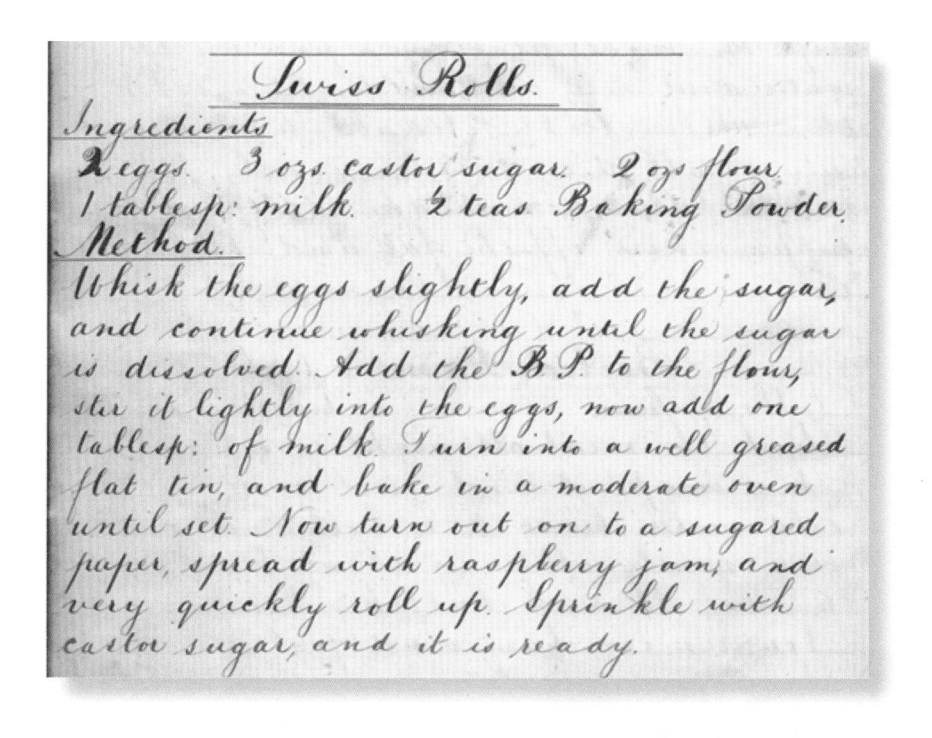

Mary's inclusion of the recipe again shows her contemporary outlook. The first references to such a cake - then called a Jelly Roll - appear in cookbooks and magazines of the 1870s. Instructions were simple : *"Bake sponge quick and while hot spread with jelly. Roll carefully, and wrap it in a cloth. When cold cut in slices for the table"*. 'Jelly' being used in the American sense of a preserve.

By the 1880s, this earlier name had been dropped, possibly due to its lewd connotations Stateside. Why 'Swiss' was substituted remains unclear. Fancy cakes filled with preserves or cream were quite a fad in Victorian times. Both Battenberg and Victoria Sponges were first formulated in the late 19th century.

Mary costs her Swiss Roll recipe at 6d: equivalent to 12 rock buns.

Lemon Mould

Lemon Mould.

2 ozs cornflour 1 pt cold water 6 ozs loaf sugar 2 lemons. yolks of 1 or 2 eggs. Mix cornflour with a little cold water, place rest of the water in a pan with the lemon rind and sugar, bring to a boil, boil 5 mins. Now strain this over the cornflour, add strained lemon juice & yolk of egg, return to the pan, stir until it boils, cook well, & then turn into a wet mould. When quite set — turn out.

Much improved if whites of eggs are whisked to a stiff froth & stirred lightly in before moulding.

'Fancy' didn't have to mean complicated. A lemon mould could be a refreshing change, and a welcome addition of vitamin C to the diet. The 'Loaf sugar' mentioned in the recipe was a cone-shaped block of sugar. This was the common way that sugar was

supplied until the end of the 19th century. Raw sugar was boiled and left to cool in inverted conical moulds, with impurities draining off through the base.

When in use, the cook scraped off the desired amount of sweetening with a knife or by using special pincers called sugar nips.

St. George's Hall Cake

This seems to be a fairly straightforward fruit cake. The reason for the specific name is unclear. There are no obvious links in the ingredients to England's patron saint and there are no halls with such a name in Rothwell. There is a St. George's Hall in Bradford, but Bradford is a long way from Rothwell, and seems to play no part in Mary's life. St. George's Hospital was a prominent feature of Rothwell life, built in the same year, 1903, that Mary began her cookbook. Unfortunately for this theory, when Mary was living in Rothwell, it was called the New Union Workhouse, only gaining the St. George's title in 1934.

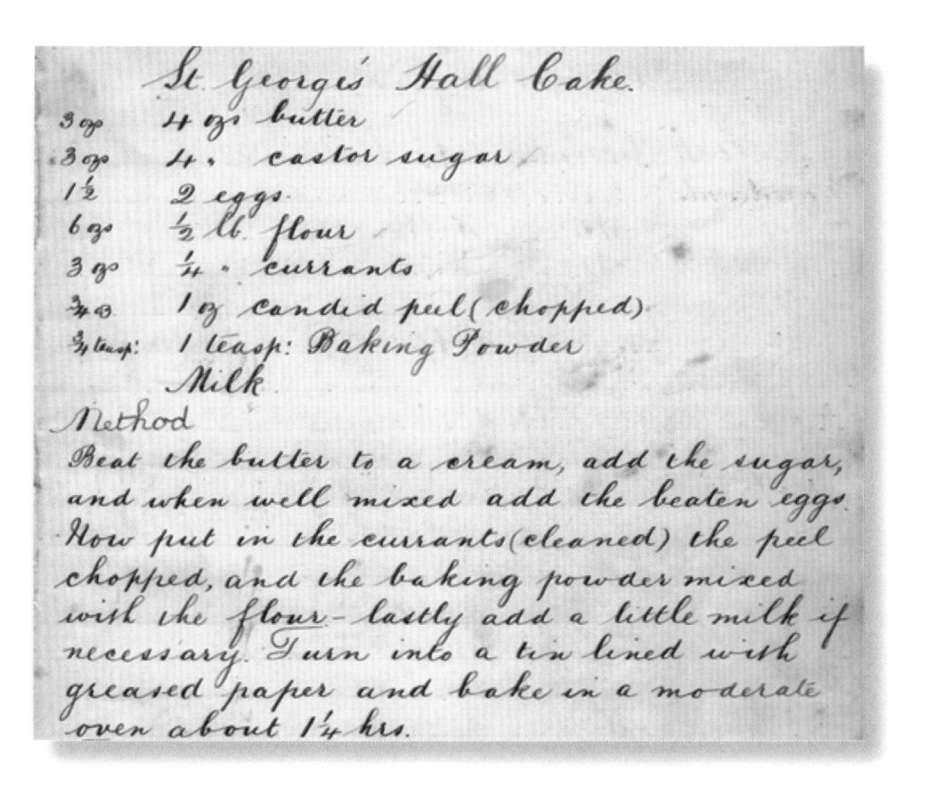

The recipe does feature in a 1911 booklet from the Liverpool School of Cookery, containing recipes that were *"most needed under all conditions and circumstances of everyday life"*. Correspondent Amy Osbourne commented that she recalled her grandmother served St. George's Hall cake as a basic fruit cake at their church in Lincoln in the 1960s if (*"something special was going on"*.

Seed Cake

Seed cake was a long-established English recipe. Mrs. Beeton mentions it, but variants of a cake containing caraway seed go back many years before that. In Chaucer's 'Canterbury Tales', the summoner, or church official, brings along a round seeded cake instead of a shield. Some old recipes maintain there is a difference between seed cake and caraway. Seed cake used yeast dough, caraway did not. As Mary's recipe doesn't include yeast it could strictly be called a caraway cake.

Thomas Tusser, in his mid-16th century book, 'Five hundred points of Good Husbandrie', rhymes to reminds the cook what she has to prepare:

Wife, sometime this week if weather is clear
An end for wheat sowing we make for this year
Remember thou therefore 'tho I do it not
The seed cake, the pasties, the frumenty pot.

Some references state that a seed cake was cooked to mark the end of the seed-sowing season, a timing which would fit with this ditty. Frumenty was based on cracked wheat boiled in sweetened milk, often made on Mothering Sunday. In a similar way to ginger cakes, the intensity of the caraway flavour increases if the cake is kept for a few days before eating.

Seed Cake

½ lb flour. 4 ozs lard or butter.
5 ozs. castor sugar.
2 teas. caraway seeds.
2 eggs. ¼ teasp! salt.
1 teasp: Baking Powder. ½ teacup milk.

Method

- Beat the butter to a cream, add the sugar, then the beaten eggs, beat well add the flour, the seeds, and lastly the milk and B.P.
Turn into a tin lined with greased paper
Bake about 1 hr. in a moderate oven.

Lastly, there has to be a fruit cake for the Festive time of year. Mary describes several similar fruit cakes, but I have chosen Mrs. Videll's recipe as it was the one that was on the scrap of paper that bore the address, "Mrs. Hall, Evening Hill". Mary's transcription was one of the last in the cookbook. One of the recipes in these later pages (not published here) has the by-line "by EH 1915". These initials could either refer to Evening Hill or to her step-daughter Evelyn Hall. We can conclude that Mary was actively recording recipes for over a decade following her evening classes of 1903. Perhaps she even asked the cooks at Cockermouth Hospital to use them.

Christmas Loaf

It seems odd that alcohol (for preservation not intoxication) is missing. Normally cakes for Christmas are prepared several weeks before the big day to allow the flavours to mature . Not including alcohol can leave a cake like this to go mouldy from the inside. The aversion to alcohol is surely not ethical : as elsewhere Mary gives a recipe for nettle beer. The cooking instructions are much vaguer, again indicating it was written for a cook who knew what she was doing rather than a student. Carrot and apple, presumably grated, were included to keep the cake moist. Hopefully the nutmeg was grated too!

This is how Mary headed her scullery section. It's clear she believes a tidy kitchen and clean utensils are vital. The second part of her syllabus states :

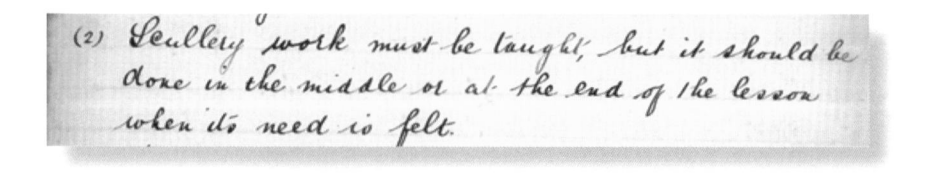

The tools she had at her disposal, and the items she had to clean, were very different from those we use today. Apart from the obvious differences such as the lack of electricity or machines such as dishwashers, many items contained materials that were much more sensitive to the' wrong kind of cleaning'.

Cutlery could have bone handles and metal utensils could be tinned or copper plated - each material with its own cleansing needs. Metal implements might need care as they had valuable surfaces such as silver plate or brass, or be made of cheap iron or steel that needed to be protected from rust, or have enamelled surfaces that mustn't be chipped.

Washing-up liquid didn't exist back then. The woman entrusted with the cleaning had a range of lotions, potions and creams to choose from, with each surface requiring its own cleaning agent.

Alkaline chemicals such as soap, soda or ammonia helped to dissolve any grease. Acid from vinegar or lemons could be useful on metal surfaces or against limescale. If a chemical treatment didn't work, sheer muscle and scouring powder were needed.

Muscle power was also needed to heft the hot water from a 'copper' heated on the fire. At the turn of the century, not all homes had a tap fed from a hot water tank. One item that was certainly essential was an endless supply of elbow grease.

Whilst Mary's students didn't have to take in all these cleaning instructions at once, the extent of physical labour and exposure to chemicals is breathtaking.

Scourers

Older readers might remember 'Vim' and 'Ajax' for enamel surfaces. Today, we still use a Brillo pad to clean metallic items. All these are ready for the kitchen worker to use. Back in Mary's day, you had to prepare your own. In Mary's kitchen, abrasives came in the form of grit and sand mixtures such as so-called Bath bricks.

> *Dripping tins to wash well in hot soapy water with soda, and scour with bath brick. Rinse*

Bath brick was a bit of a funny name, as the town of Bath is famous for being made of stone. The bricks actually come from Bridgwater in Somerset, where it was found that silt from the River Perrett had just the right mixture of alumina and sand to make a household cleaner. The silt was fired in the same way as a normal brick - but for less time and at a lower temperature. When the brick was to be used in the kitchen, part of the solid was ground down to either use as a powder (see Mary's advice on forks, below) to sharpen, or into a paste (as above) to clean. It was like having one's own ready supply of sandpaper.

> *Rub forks with powdered bathbrick being careful to clean well between prongs, & dust*

Bath brick was hugely successful in the 19th century, with over 24 million being fired. It was widely used in the British Army. The advertising line was : *"the most effective and economical polishing material. It is superior to metal polish and does not contain acid or alcohol injurious to metals.".*

So, whilst unfamiliar to us today, Bath brick would have been well known to Mary's students.

A Bath brick. Courtesy Somerset Brick and Tile Museum

A second kind of scourer was a new kind of cleansing bar called 'Monkey Soap'

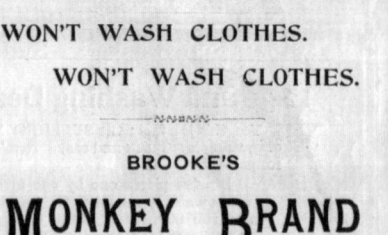

WON'T WASH CLOTHES.

WON'T WASH CLOTHES.

BROOKE'S

MONKEY BRAND

SOAP

FOR KITCHEN TABLES AND FLOORS,
LINOLEUM AND OILCLOTHS.

For Polishing Metals, Marble, Paint, Cutlery, Crockery,
Machinery, Baths, Stair-Rods.

FOR STEEL, IRON, BRASS AND COPPER VESSELS,
FIRE-IRONS, MANTELS, &c.

REMOVES RUST, DIRT, STAINS, TARNISH, &c.

In 1903, this was quite a new product for use in the kitchen making its debut for the Benjamin Brooke company in 1899, then taken on by Lever Bros, who are still in the cleaning business today. The unusual advertising slogan, *"won't wash clothes"*, advised the housewife not to add this monkey to the wash tub. A wise instruction as Monkey Soap was a coarse cleanser containing pumice stone embedded in the soap. Today we use this to rub dry skin off heels and elbows. So the monkey was perfect for cleaning metal, but perhaps a little robust for collars and cuffs.

Mary advises Monkey soap for iron utensils

Iron spoons. Wash to remove grease. Rub with moistened Monkey Soap or bath-brick Polish well with dry whitening. Wash & dry

'Whitening' is still with us today in toothpaste. In that use, it's normally powdered calcium carbonate or chalk dust, ground down to make a gentle abrasive to rub a surface clean, and mildly alkaline to dissolve any greasy residue.

Hot water and soap

At the turn of the 20th century, houses had begun to have hot water cylinders fitted, sometimes as back boilers behind the range. Mary draws a diagram of such an arrangement when she describes a range. This is shown in chapter 6. If that was the case, all the fortunate cook had to do was to draw off the hot water from the tap and bring it across to the sink.

If not, the water would have to be heated via a separate 'copper' or via a large pan or kettle on the hob. The soap in the soapy water that Mary refers to was probably plant-based "soft soap" rather than carbolic. Soda could be either sodium hydroxide or the milder sodium carbonate. Both remain available today.

A copper kettle for producing the hot water (if it wasn't plumbed in), a copper pail to carry it to where it was needed, and a Belfast sink with wooden drainer for the washing up

This display of kitchen equipment shows some more of the items that might have been utensils in a kitchen of Mary's time :

From left to right:

Kettle, resting on a wooden slatted stool that a child might stand on whilst watching mother cook.
Pan scales
Brass weights
Preserving pan
Rotating Mouli grinder
Carving knife and fork and bone handled table cutlery
Hand mincer
Baking powder
Flour scoop with some lentils
Colander
Weights for scales
These are all resting on a well-scrubbed wooden table.

Doing the washing up

Methodical as always, Mary instructs her students to clean things in the right order. First the glass and crockery.

> **Washing up.**
> Collect dirty things, and put those of a kind together.
> Remove all bits and slops.
> Wash the glass.
> **Crockery.**
> 1. Wash in hot soapy water.
> 2. Rinse in fresh hot water.
> 3. Drain and dry well.

No chemicals needed there, but now for the cutlery. In Mary's kitchen, it's not just a matter of keeping things clean : part of the job was to keep the blades and tines sharp and fit for purpose. Knife machines passed the blade between abrasive blocks.

> **Washing knives and forks.**
> Put in a jug of hot water with soap keeping the handles out of the water.
> Rinse and dry well.
> **Cleaning.**
> Rub knives on board with powdered bathbrick, until clean & bright. dust, or clean on knife machine.
> Rub forks with powdered bathbrick being careful to clean well between prongs, & dust.

> Knives and forks must be washed in hot soapy water, but the handles must be kept out of the water, or the handles will come loose.
> Iron spoons. Wash to remove grease. Rub with moistened Monkey Soap or bath-brick Polish well with dry whitening. Wash & dry

After the glasses, crocks and cutlery, it was time for the pans!

II Washing and Cleaning Pans, Skewers and Tins.

Washing all kinds of Pans.

After using all pans fill at once with hot water, and if food has stuck or burnt on, add soda to water and boil.

Sauce pans - iron.

Wash out well with hot soapy water. Scour well with pan mixture. Rinse. Dry.

Enamelled. Wash with hot soapy water scour with egg shells, and salt, or pan mixture.

Omelet. After using, wipe well with paper. Then rub with damp hot dishcloth, and dry. If very dirty treat like ordinary pans.

Dripping tins wash well in hot soapy water, with soda, and scour with bath-brick. Rinse and dry.

Polishing tins. Wash to remove grease and dry. Rub over with moistened whitening, and dry.

Points to be remembered.

1. All pans must be washed and scoured inside and outside.

2. If the food has stuck on the pans, something gritty must be used. viz bathbrick or sand, or boiled with water & soda.

3. If very greasy use soda as well as soap. in the water.

4. Thoroughly dry all pans, before putting away.

Mary suggests her own 'pan mixture' to supplement Bath brick. 'Calais' sand was a very fine sand, sometimes (but hopefully not in Mary's case) used alongside sulphuric acid in cleaning metal. It seems to be just another abrasive to be used with soap, and it's not clear why Mary chooses to make her own mixture rather than using Bath brick or Monkey Soap.

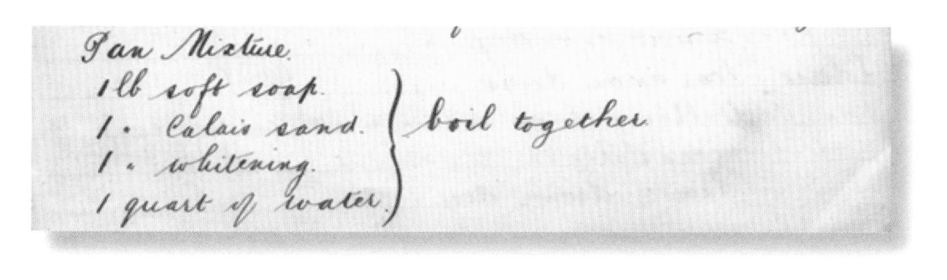

Whilst the use of all these abrasive chemicals and scouring materials is described in detail, it's instructive to see that there's no mention of any protection for the kitchen maid's hands. With all this scouring and degreasing going on, it's a worry what will happen to the complexion!

After making use of the sink, now it must be cleaned. More hot water and scrubbing!

From context, we must assume that most of Mary's students' kitchens had running water, a supply of hot water on tap and mains drainage. These were relatively recent innovations. Mains water became commonplace in the early part of the 20th century. The Public Health Act of 1890 meant proper drainage became more widespread and the practice of throwing slops out into a back yard was thankfully dying out.

Mary is also thorough enough to remind her students that they need to keep the pipes flowing cleanly all the way to the main drain - another example of her modern thinking.

Now for any metallic utensils. Mary warns her students against gritty 'plate powder'. However, Goddard's of Leicester's non-mercurial 'Plate Powder', first introduced in the 1840s, had a good reputation as an effective and non-scratching cleaner for silver.

Brass   Copper.   Silver
1. Brass and Copper: Wash everything free from grease.
2. Use an acid with salt to remove stains.
3. After rubbing with paste, allow it to dry to prevent smearing
4. Use something gritty to remove rust or burnt marks
5. After using a moistened paste, polish well with whitening or flour to prevent tarnishing
Silver.
Wash in very hot soapy water to remove grease. Rinse in very hot water, drain, & dry on soft clean towel.
Once a week, rub over with moistened plate powder. Rub off with soft rag
Polish with leather
Brush out all crevices to free from powder
Never use plate powder, which is gritty or silver will be scratched.

Rub off powder with cloth.
Polish with dry whitening & leather.
Brush crevices.

Then there are the work surfaces and any machines that have been in use.

Boards & Tables.
1. Rub over with wet dishcloth.
2. Scrub with soap & water, & a very little sand
3. Rinse very well and dry.

Mincing Machine.
1. Unscrew handle & pull to pieces, Soak well
3. Wash thoroughly in hot soapy water, rinse and dry.
4. When quite dry, put together again.

And don't forget, after you've used the cloths to clean the kitchen, you have to clean the cloths themselves. No throw-away paper towels or cheap sponges here! Hartshorn contains ammonia, a milder alkali than soda, in Mary's day made from antlers of deer. Ammonia is another kitchen chemical still used today to clean kitchen surfaces, but coming from industrial rather than biological sources.

Polishing Cloths.
1 oz of Hartshorn Powder. 1 pint of milk
Boil the cloths in it for 5 mins. Rinse quickly & dry.

Oh, and before you finish, remember...

Note.
1. Do not use soda when washing wooden things or they will become a bad colour.
2. Scrub wood way of grain or it will become rough.
3. After using sand for boards, rinse very well
4. Allow air to circulate well round wooden things whilst drying.

And after all that, I think Mary's student is entitled to put her feet up - having given the hands a good treatment of moisturizing cream!

Proprietary mixtures still available today such as Ponds Cream existed in 1903, or perhaps simply rubbing some Vaseline into the complexion would revive the skin after exposure to all that grit and grease-dissolving solvents.

Vaseline was first produced by the Chesebrough Manufacturing Company in 1876, and was the first cold cream made with mineral oil and petroleum jelly. Pond's Cold Cream, containing witch hazel extract in an alcoholic solution, had also been available since a slightly earlier date.

Durability, efficiency, economy

At the end of her cleaning instructions, Mary considers the attributes of a good gas cooker. The diagram is in chapter 7 and at the end of her copperplate writing, there is a brief but authoritative pencilled note : "*Essential features of a good stove: Durability, efficiency, economy*".

This trio of worthy attributes admirably sum up what Mary expected of her students when they were in the kitchen, and indeed her entire approach to working life in the kitchen, pantry and scullery.

Putting Mary's Book in its Context

To fully appreciate Mary's work, in addition to her life story, recipes and kitchen management, I feel it's important to write a little about the kind of kitchen equipment Mary's students might have had, the kind of meals that they might be expected to cook and how Domestic Science was taught. Mary had a ready audience. In 1903, around 20 000 people lived in the Rothwell area, which was close to active pits with their associated industries, and connected to the railway system. Plenty of labourer's daughters and factory girls keen to benefit from culinary advice! Rothwell also had some fine houses whose occupants would no doubt be glad that their domestic servants could learn new skills.

Shopping

To cook you need provisions. Domestic servants may have worked in a household that had new-fangled appliances such as gas-fired stoves and refrigerators. These, along with tinned meat, had all begun to be seen in the UK in the years before Mary wrote her book.

But studying Mary's recipes shows, in the most part, she was devising meals with an eye to the working-class, physical labourers such as she would have known on her family's farms, and from Levi Rowley's work. For the majority of her students, it was a matter of a daily shop and eking out the allowance from the weekly pay packet.

Commercial Street in Rothwell, and the roads that led off it, had a good supply of butchers, bakers and greengrocers. The Co-operative store, demolished in the 1960s, was a source not only of goods but also the 'divi' or dividend. This was a small percentage of the cost price credited to the shopper, which built up, with repeated purchases, to a useful sum to be cashed in for high days and holidays.

If a visit to the shops was not possible, then a call from travelling butchers, fishmongers or muffin men would be welcome. The milkman also made a daily round. In Rothwell, milk was delivered, still warm, direct from the local farm, costing 2d (1p) per pint, or 1d for yesterday's. The milk was sold via graduated ladles extracting it from churns into earthenware pitchers.

Back in 1903, market day stalls could bring a fresher, and wider range of ingredients. Rothwell has a Market Cross and a Charter going back to 1408. Although there has not been a regular Saturday market in the town for at least 20 years, in 1903 it would have been a regular shopping destination for Mary's students. Market stalls used the area of waste ground near to Mary's lodgings in Steel Terrace.

Above : Rothwell's Church, Maypole, modern Market Cross and supermarket at the top end of Commercial Street, 2015

Below : 1960s flats crowd around Steel Terrace on the former area of waste ground that used to host Rothwell Feast and a weekly market. Picture taken in 2015.

Storage

Leaving aside the few households that had a fridge, and the occasions when fresh fish would come with ice, the competent cook tried to store her food in dark, cool but airy conditions. These were the requisite conditions for a good pantry.

Meat was kept in a meat safe. This was a wooden box with cool marble shelves or slatted wooden ones to allow for movement of air. The metallic mesh door acted against flies whilst allowing air to circulate. If the meat was going a little 'green', application of a vinegar-soaked cloth could save the situation. Sometimes dairy products were kept in the safe too, in which case, care had to be taken to avoid cross-contamination.

Bread was kept in an earthenware bread crock. This also aimed to keep the food cool, and allow airflow to avoid mould forming, but with a lid to stop mice getting in.

The milk supplied might not have been heat-treated. Gentle boiling on the range followed by cooling in the pitcher before a return to the pantry, could extend the useful life of the milk. If it was in danger of going off, it could be used up in a dish like rice pudding.

Potatoes and root vegetables needed to be stored in dark and dry areas, well away from mice. Fruit was eaten in season, or bottled, jammed or candied to preserve it.

Meat safe and a bread crock

Above : Preserving pan and a tin of Leeds Industrial Co-op baking powder

The range

The cook needed a full range of culinary skills and the instrument on which she had to use them was, appropriately enough, called the 'range'. Modern kitchens may have their Agas or Rayburns: the Edwardian range was similarly designed for a variety of cooking processes. In Mary's time, ranges were largely solid-fuel fired, but some houses had begun to have town gas versions installed.

A coal-fired range would have to have the ashes emptied out each morning and a fresh fire laid and lit before any thought could be given to high-temperature cooking. A matt black finish produced the greatest heat efficiency, so, once cleaned, the range had to be 'black leaded' on a regular basis.

The Yorkshire cast-iron 'open' range had a central fire exposed to the kitchen. This heated the oven to its side, but was also handy for roasting or toasting. Some ranges had a set of bars that could fold down over the fire for pots and pans, and might have a boiler to the other side of the fire to heat water.

The solid-fuel hob was the regular home for a kettle full of water boiling away alongside the simmering stock pot cooking bones for a broth or rooty veg for a hearty stew. Steamed puddings could make use of the heat of the boiling water too.

A typical Yorkshire Range

The closed versions or 'kitcheners' had a hotplate or hob over the fire and 'rings', as on today's cookers. Metal plates could be slid in front of the fire to redirect heat to the oven or hob. Mary sketched a diagram of this kind of range, with a boiler or 'set pot' for hot water to the rear, and two ovens, to help her students work efficiently. Most of the parts are self explanatory, but the 'dampers' referred to controlled the flow of air through the flues, and so the amount of heat produced.

A range could cook meat in many ways. Boiling used the stock pot, and any meat for frying went in a suitably greased pan on the hob. Roasting on a range meant spit roasting not, as we currently do, baking in an oven, so an open fire was needed. To reach the temperature required, the cook had to build up the fire a half hour or so in advance, and then turn the joint by hand, just as adventurous types nowadays attempt on modern barbecues. Preserving pans also used the hob. The best ones were made of copper as it conducts heat well to allow long slow cooking of the spiced and sugary fruit mixture. In the meantime the sterilized glass jars would be drying off in the oven.

In the vicinity of the range would be a plethora of hooks to hang pans and kettles, cloths to hold the pan handles, a poker and shovel to tend to the fire, water jugs and essentials such as salt, tea and biscuits.

Looking after the gas-fired range

Mary also described how to service a gas-fired range.

The gas used to power such a range was not today's 'North Sea' gas, or methane, but 'town' or 'coal' gas - a mixture of hydrogen, methane and the highly poisonous carbon monoxide. That's where the old threat of killing yourself by *'putting your head in the gas oven'* comes from. As the monoxide burns with a clean blue flame Mary advises that the cook should "*See that the flame is non-luminous, and makes no noise or smell in burning*". She also notes there should be no smoke - if there was that would mean the carbon in the fuel had not fully burnt, meaning inefficient heating.

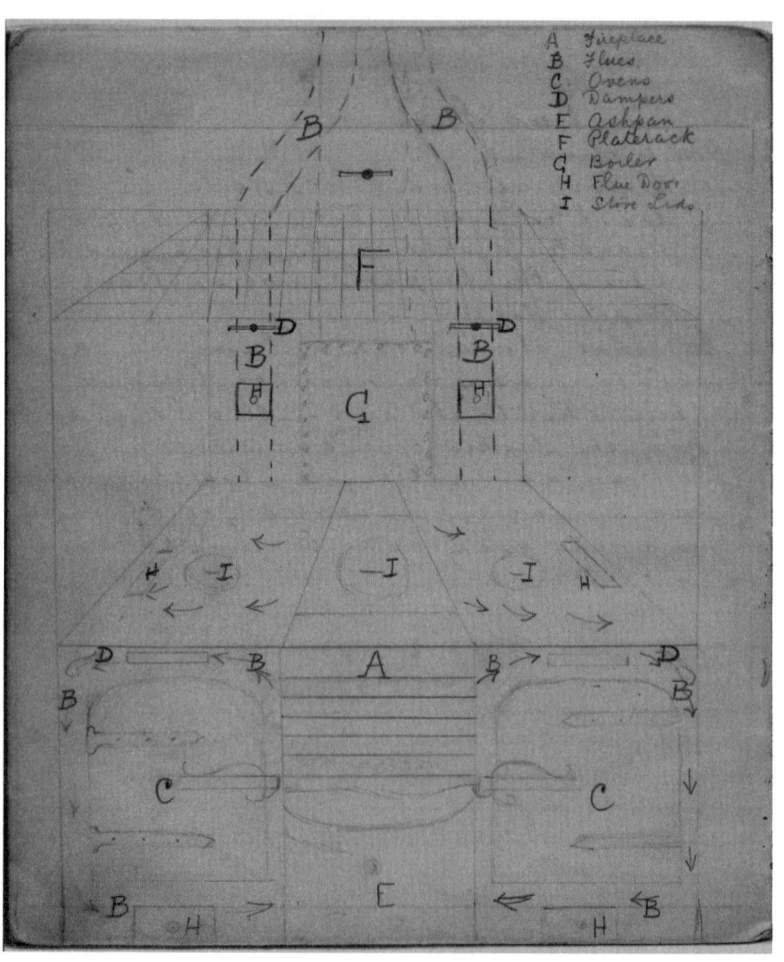

Mary's diagram of a range

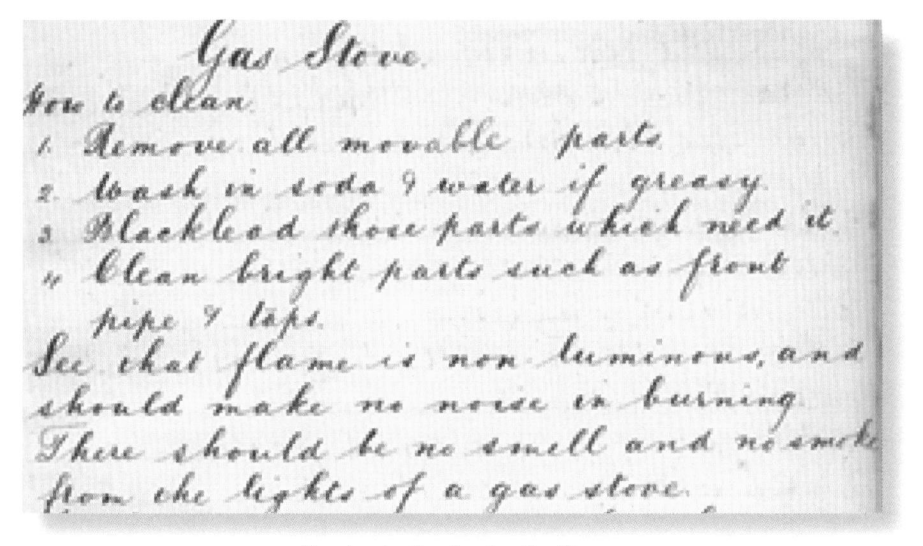

Mary's rules for cleaning Gas Stoves

What else might be in the kitchen?

At the centre of the kitchen would be a solid wooden table. Large enough for the cook to do her work in preparing food, it was also where the family ate, where children played or learnt, as well as acting as ironing board, once the cast iron, flat 'irons' had been heated on the hotplate. Unless washing was drying there, plates could dry and be warmed above the range. Other crockery, utilitarian bowls, jugs, dishes and pots, dining and meat plates filled the shelves and cupboards of a dresser or sideboard. Some food may have been stored there too.

To measure quantities for cooking, a set of scales and brass weights were essential.

A flour scoop came in handy for transferring powders or pulses to the scale pan.

Finally, a kitchen sink was needed for washing and food preparation. This would probably be an earthenware, rectangular 'Belfast sink' with a wooden drainer, as shown in chapter 6.

Brass scales, weights and flour scoop

What kind of food did people eat?

Seebohm Rowntree famously surveyed the living conditions of working class families in York in the late 19th century, a time and location similar to the ones in which Mary composed her cookbook.

Rowntree found that breakfast centred on bread and butter or dripping, with possibly a scraping of jam or treacle. A rasher of bacon, a couple of sausages or a portion of porridge or boiled eggs might accompany the bread. Tea was the universal drink of choice.

Dinner, around noon, was the most substantial meal of the day. On Sundays, the housewife would have time to prepare a roast with vegetables, and the family had time to sit down and enjoy it. Yorkshire pudding was vital in bulking out the meal. In many families, a pudding as large as the plate was served first to fill empty stomachs so that less of the finer fare was needed to sate the appetite.

Chapter 4 detailed several uses that Mary suggested for cold meat leftovers. As well as these, in summer, meat could just be served cold with pickles.

For the latter part of the week, the main source of protein could be cheaper meats such as liver or rabbit; preserved and pressed meat such as brawn, haslet or faggots, or tripe and chitterlings. If times were really hard, just a Yorkshire with gravy might have to be the main meal.

Alternatively a soup or broth, based on stock from bones or giblets or from well-soaked peas or lentils, could be served. Yet more bread spread with fat provided necessary bulk. Mary's regular use of lard and dripping has been commented on in chapter 4. 'Fish on Friday' was common, for both religious and nutritious reasons.

The late afternoon or early evening saw a lighter meal : more tea and bread, but if the budget could stretch to it, tea cakes, custard tarts, a bit of salad and maybe some jam on the bread. Puddings generally took the form of slow-cooked rice or sago puddings or fruit pies and tarts. However, the relatively high cost of sugar deterred poorer housewives from making a sweet dessert, so sometimes pudding was just a Yorkshire with jam. Oddly, Mary's book does not contain jam-making recipes.

A man also needed his 'relish' - not a sauce, but something a bit extra for supper : an egg, a rasher of bacon or a small piece of cheese or fish, to keep him in good condition to earn the family's weekly income.

It's to Mary's credit that her cookbook and lessons describe a much more adventurous diet than the one that Rowntree observed. She shows that varied and nutritious meals could be produced, whilst still sticking to a strict budget.

How did Mary's lessons fit in with education in 1903?

Mary's book is dated 1903, meaning that if she started teaching her classes at that time, it was a moment when English education was undergoing huge change. A full description of those changes is beyond the scope of this book, but it's important to put Mary's work in context and to realise how modern her ideas were.

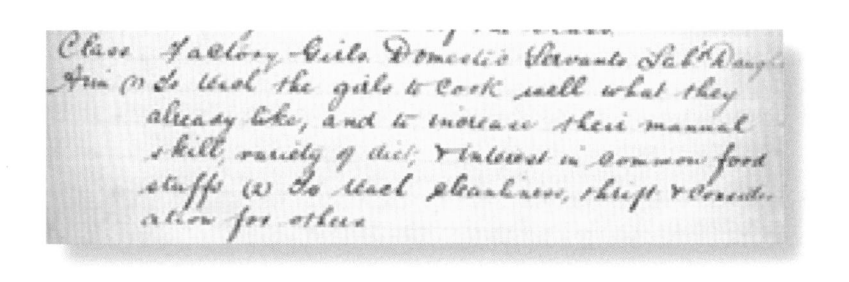

Her careful planning of lessons, and the desire to make her lessons meaningful and useful to all the women she taught, mark Mary out to be someone very much at the forefront of teaching Domestic Science. The quality of Mary's work in this sphere is another reason why it is important that extracts from her book are published.

During the previous fifty years, public debate and a series of Acts of Parliament had gradually made education free and compulsory for children between 5 and 13 years of age, and the role of Domestic Science education had gradually increased in prominence.

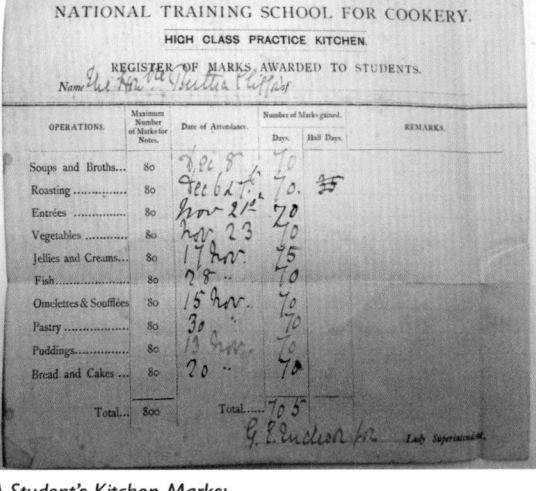

A Student's Kitchen Marks:
Courtesy emscote.co.uk

In 1873 a series of lectures on the scientific principles of cooking were given at South Kensington in London. These were wildly successful, with one critic noting that the lectures were "*far more interesting than most plays these days*". Shades of the success of the 'Great British Bake Off' 140 years later!

A prospectus for a National School of Cookery was issued. Its aim was to "*teach the best methods of cooking...food in general consumption amongst all classes*"

However, the appropriate approach was not clear. In simple terms, some favoured the idea that well-trained 'ladies' would have the appropriate skills to teach the lower classes, whilst the opposing view was that technical expertise in the kitchen on the part of the teacher was a more valuable skill.

Careers advice in the 1880s presented elementary teaching as the best a working-class girl could aspire to, but the field of Domestic Science was *"suitable for a middle-class woman's social conscience"*. However, recruits from Domestic Science training schools could sometimes not have the appropriate attitude. A correspondent to the journal 'Education' noted, *"She has a vague notion that there exists an uninteresting class of oft-times dirty and poorly-dressed folk who...she regards as common, but of the individual artisan, his habits and family life and requirements she knows nothing"*.

Contrast that to Mary's inclusive approach and desire to tailor her lessons to the needs of her students and their families: *"To teach the girls to cook well what they already like"*.

There was also disagreement between Church schools and non-denominational, or 'Board' schools.

This was a much more serious split than it may seem now, as church-going was a central aspect of life at the turn of the 20th century. Most Anglican clergy, and many parishioners, were strongly opposed to Board schools, especially if such a school replaced one with a strong Anglican ethos. In contrast, many non-conformists welcomed the provision of non-denominational education through a ratepayer-funded board school. This division was a source of local tensions. Eventually, in 1902, a new Act abolished these arrangements and set up Local Education Authorities; the LEAs we still have today.

The matter of what was to be taught in schools also came into question. The 19th century class was still dominated by Latin, Greek and Religious Studies, with literacy, numeracy and subjects such as geography and sciences only being taught to a basic level. Thankfully, the relevance of Domestic Science gradually became apparent.

The point was well made in an article in the 'Manchester Guardian' in September 1901where it is stated, *"Perhaps in time it will become customary to allow a year at the close of a girl's school life for the careful and systematic acquisition of domestic knowledge"*.

The article continues : *"The combination of careless methods and downright waste which passes for cookery among the poorer classes needs a determined attack if it is to be exterminated, and the school period, young as it is, affords the only chance."*

Mary's proposed lessons, thrifty household management, and the kind of audience she hoped to address, again echoes the 'Guardian' article, which concludes, "*In another twenty years we may look back with amazement at the want of foresight which left preparation for the complex and exacting task of household management almost wholly to chance.*"

"*The problem of servants, which is fast appropriating to itself the title of 'the domestic difficulty,' makes familiarity with household arts almost imperative in the mistress.*"

Whilst Mary's lessons were aimed at an older age range than the girls in compulsory education, and for an Evening Class rather than lessons during the normal school day, her quality and modern approach shine through.

She plans thoroughly, attempts to make her lessons relevant and useful to her class and draws on contemporary sources to deliver the most modern education available. Such praiseworthy attitudes are as applicable in 2016 as they were in 1903.

As Mary states in her own syllabus ...

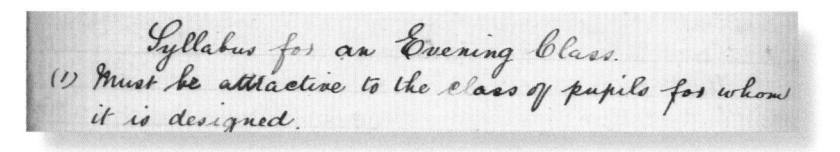

... and the point at the very top of her list is a very modern sentiment indeed.

Leaving to one side the intrigue of her life story and the quality and variety of her recipes, I'm very pleased to have been able to publish Mary's work as that of a woman who is so clearly ahead of her times in wanting the best for her 'sisters' who slaved in front of the range and over the sink.

Thanks

This book would not have been possible without the help of many individuals and organizations. I'm grateful for all their help.

For publicity in the search for Mary : 'Selby Times' and 'Cumberland Times' newspapers ; 'Down Your Way', 'Howden Matters' and 'Rothwell Record' magazines; Radio Humberside.

For historical research : Selby Library; Cumbria Archives; Cumbria Bereavement Department; Cockermouth Heritage Group; Goole Library; the London Gazette.

For historic kitchen equipment : Ian and Dorothy Pattison.

For individual assistance, research and comment : Susan Butler; Claire Crossdale; Linda Gowans; Hazel Martell; Amy Osbourne; Diana Parsons; Dorothy Pattison; Angela Swann; David Winpenny; Dorothy Woodall.

For Blakey family information and images : Jane and Tim Long; Susan Blakey.

For proof reading : Hazel Allison; Dorothy Pattison; Angela Swann.

For cooking samples of the cakes: Sara Mackay at 'The Hub', Selby.

For printing : Axis Print, Brighouse.

For support, advice, cookery and encouragement : Mary Lewis, Elspeth Lewis.

And of course, most importantly of all, the anonymous benefactor who donated the book in the first place!

The images are mine unless noted otherwise. For those other images, they have either been declared copyright free, or their owners have given permission for use, for which I am grateful. In these cases, I have noted the owners' name next to the image. In a couple of cases, images have been obtained online, but whilst I have tried to contact their owners, I've had no success. If there are any problems in this respect, please contact me as below. The use of images in this book does not imply permission to use any images elsewhere.

Having had the help and advice of all those mentioned above, I take full responsibility for remaining errors and mistakes.

Should people wish to suggest improvements or have further information on Mary Eleanor, again, please contact me via the address on page 107.

Books, Webpage and Picture Credits (where not stated in text)

Eliza Acton : 'Modern Cookery for Private Families' (1845)
Martin Bairstow : 'Railways around Harrogate' (1986)
Isabella Beeton : 'Everyday Cookery' (as adapted, 1972)
Maggie Black : 'Food and cooking in 19th century Britain' (1985)
Peter Brears : 'Traditional Food in Yorkshire' (1987)
Laura Mason and Catherine Brown : 'The Taste of Britain' (2006)
Annmarie Turnbull : 'An Isolated Missionary: The Domestic Subjects Teacher in England,1870-1914' Women's' History Review, Vol. 3, No. 1 (1994)

General advice on foods : www.foodsofengland.co.uk
Wikipedia - and links from it - as an encyclopaedia

Olney Pancakes : www.rswoodford.co.uk/year7/lentshrove.html
Swiss Rolls : Mary Gage 'Jelly Roll' : www.newenglandrecipes.org/html/jelly-roll.html
Birds Custard image : 'Star1950' on flickr
Alfred Bird cemetery : Friends of Key Hill Cemetery : www.fkwc.org/
Oldroyd's Rhubarb/rhubarb tours : www.yorkshirerhubarb.co.uk/
Rhubarb Festival : www.wakefield.gov.uk/rhubarb
Sugar nips : Hamster62 via Wikimedia
Sugar loaf scraping : https://pepyssmallchange.wordpress.com/2015/02/15/mr-dry-at-the-three-sugar-loaves-in-wapping/
Vaseline image : www.cosmeticsandskin.com
Rothwell History : www.leeds.gov.uk/docs/rothwell%20conservation%20area%20 appraisal%20and%20management%20plan%20final.pdf
Crackenthorpe Hall : www.visitcumbria.com
Crackenthorpe Hall history : http://archaeologydataservice.ac.uk/archiveDS/ archiveDownload?t=arch-20551/dissemination/pdf/Article_Level_Pdf/ tcwaas/002/1933/vol33/tcwaas_002_1933_vol33_0011.pdf
Ripon Rowel route : www.gpsroutes.co.uk/routes/home.nsf/ osmapdisp?openform&route=ripon-rowel-walking-route
Walk passing Whipley Hall : www.thenorthernecho.co.uk/resources/files/34224/

David Lewis : dglmeb@gmail.com : Selby, February 2016.